Healing the Inner Child

How You Can Begin to Heal the Wounded Soul Within Using Meditation, Awareness, Journaling, and More

Your Free Gift
(only available for a limited time)

Thanks for getting this book! If you want to learn more about various spirituality topics, then join Mari Silva's community and get a free guided meditation MP3 for awakening your third eye. This guided meditation mp3 is designed to open and strengthen ones third eye so you can experience a higher state of consciousness. Simply visit the link below the image to get started.

https://spiritualityspot.com/meditation

Table of Contents

Introduction

"Do we ever really grow up?"

We ponder this question every once in a while, sometimes during a joke or a serious conversation. However, it doesn't matter how old we are or how mature we feel; our inner child is always lurking, hoping to be heard and felt. We want to give you a chance to get acquainted with your inner child with the help of this book.

We understand that some people may not be familiar with the term "inner child." The topic may also be a little sensitive, especially if you have experienced something traumatic your inner child is still suffering from. For this reason, we made sure to take a simple approach and treat this subject with the level of sensitivity it deserves. We didn't want to use complicated terminologies like other books on the market that alienate the reader. We put so much thought into writing this book. We decided to use a more understanding and humane tone than the other available books.

We want the reader to look at their inner child with love and understanding to be able to contain their pain. Your inner child isn't a disease symptom; you can't just take a pill to numb its pain. It is a part of you that requires a different type of healing. This is why we have included hands-on methods and instructions to help you with the healing process. All the methods mentioned in this book have proven multiple times to be successful for all kinds of different people. These instructions are clear and to the point to avoid confusion and make it easy for you to follow them step by step.

"What is an inner child?"

This is the question that brought you here. However, the answer isn't just a simple definition you can easily find on Google. There is more to this question, and we provided a detailed answer without making it too complicated. We will cover everything related to the concept of an inner child to help you learn more about yourself.

When you become aware of your trauma and come face to face with your pain, you will be able to heal and grow. However, you should first discover your inner child and learn to accept it, as this is the only way you can begin the healing process. In this book, we will help you take these steps so you can finally grow and let go of your past wounds.

No one said the healing journey is easy. However, it begins with one single step that will put you in the right direction. By reading this book, you are taking your first steps on the journey of healing so you can let go of the past and grow into the best version of yourself. Take a long deep breath, relax, and be ready to meet your inner child.

Chapter 1: The Inner Child Explained

As children, we couldn't wait to grow up and become adults. We have always believed that adulthood is much more fun. You don't live with your parents anymore; you become financially independent and are in charge of your own decisions. You live life on your own terms and experience the freedom that comes with being a grown-up. However, one day your boss gives you a negative evaluation, or you have a huge fight with your best friend, and suddenly, you are back to your six-year-old self. You just want to cry or throw a tantrum and hope for someone to hold you tight and tell you, "Everything will be ok."

It's important to understand what your inner child is.
https://unsplash.com/photos/EwfrjhOGvtY

What brought these feelings on? This is most likely your inner child coming out of hiding and trying to tell you something. So, what is an inner child? Where has this term come from?

The Inner Child

Psychiatrist Carl Jung first coined the term inner child. After spending some time working on his inner self and trying to understand the reasons behind his childlike emotions, Jung made this discovery. He realized that another part of our personality impacts our actions and decisions. Jung called it "the inner child" to describe the part inside of us that has not grown up and is still stuck in the childhood stage. Some emotions and memories still haunt us and are played like a movie inside our heads, while there are other happy ones that we fondly reminisce about. All of these memories and experiences, whether good or bad, are stored in the unconscious and create the inner child.

The word child always goes hand in hand with innocence, joy, and a carefree attitude. Although the inner child stores these positive emotions and characteristics, it also stores all the negativity, trauma, and pain you suffered in the hands of those you loved and trusted the most, like your parents or teachers. In fact, our personalities begin to shape from three to five years old. Unfortunately, you don't get over these feelings, and they stay with you, influencing your decisions, relationships, and other aspects of your life.

Because of its name, the term "inner child" is sometimes used lightly. Unlike what some people may believe, this term doesn't mean having childish thoughts or acting like a child. It is an aspect of our personality that exists in our unconscious and can be described as a "subpersonality." Simply put, this is another side of your personality that usually comes out when you face adversity.

When your inner child takes over, you make decisions, have thoughts, and display certain behaviors based on your childhood trauma and your inner child's need to protect you. Your inner child isn't aware that you have grown up and your life has changed. Your unmet needs and repressed emotions show up when you least expect them in the form of anger, rebellion, or fear. You may still hold on to certain thoughts and beliefs engraved in your brain since you were a child, like sex is taboo or boys don't cry.

Your past trauma will make your soul heavy due to all the pain and negativity you carry. Every decision you make is driven by fear and the desire to protect yourself from things that aren't real or no longer impact your life.

Your inner child is a wounded soul that was abused emotionally, physically, or both. Maybe your family was emotionally abusive, or you were bullied as a child at home or school, or you were raised by narcissistic parents who couldn't love you the way every child wants to be loved. Just like your body can be covered with wounds after an accident, so can your soul after a traumatic upbringing. However, unlike physical wounds that heal over time, soul wounds don't heal, and your inner child never grows or develops. The pain you have experienced can grow with you, and if you don't take the necessary steps to heal, you will suffer for the rest of your life.

It is vital for your well-being that you become aware of your inner child. Some people may experience tantrums or angry outbursts like a child and have no idea what triggered these emotions. Learning about your inner child and working on yourself will help you heal and experience spiritual awakening and growth. Uncovering your past experiences and understanding the root of your pain and fears will put you on your road to healing.

Although your inner child is the product of your past experiences, it plays a huge role in shaping your personality as an adult. Instead of letting it shape you into someone angry, hurt, or bitter, you can let it help you move on from your past and forgive yourself and others. You can become a more confident person, knowing who you are and what you want. You can finally get to experience the fun and creative part of your inner child now that it is no longer consumed with negativity.

When you experience healing, a weight will be lifted off your shoulder as your soul heals, your spirit awakens, and you experience spiritual growth. You are no longer controlled by fear or trauma.

According to coach and author Cheryl Richardson, "Inner Child work is essential. It's the essence of growth as a whole person." You won't be able to change and let go of the past holding you back and become the person you have always wanted to be if you don't work on your inner child first. Working on it will help you get over your childhood pain and trauma. You will be able to make decisions based on your adult experience instead of childhood fears.

How Is Your Inner Child Shaped?

As mentioned, your inner child is shaped by all your childhood memories and experiences, the good and the bad. It remembers how happy you were when your dad would pick you up from school and take you and your siblings to your favorite pizza place or how happy your grandpa's smile made you every time you came to visit. These things fill you with love and warmth every time you reminisce over these memories. It also remembers how you were the only one in your class that wasn't invited to a birthday party. Your inner child still remembers your mother's pain when she got the news that your grandma passed away. Every single time a kid at school called you a name or made fun of is still engraved in your memories.

It still remembers how your childhood best friend decided one day they didn't want to be friends because you weren't cool anymore or the time your teacher embarrassed you in front of the whole class. It remembers if a parent was physically, mentally, or emotionally abusive or unavailable. How they made you lose faith in your looks every time they tell you to lose weight or make comments about your body when you eat pizza or a chocolate bar.

You grow up a little and reach the awkward teen years. Your inner child is still there, filled with self-doubt as a result of your upbringing. It is with you during your first job interview, afraid, because it still remembers all the time your parents made you feel like you weren't good enough. It shows up when you and your partner fight; you fear they will abandon you just like your parents did or won't think you are good enough - perhaps like your mom or dad made you feel.

Your inner child is shaped by everything you have ever experienced, seen, heard, and felt. All your positive and negative experiences influence who you are today. Even the smallest things your parents taught you to, like how you should stay in your job even if you hate it or you should put make-up on, or no one will look at you. Simply put, your inner child is shaped by your entire childhood. Even the experiences you may not remember are still living in your unconscious mind, triggering you.

Other childhood experiences that shaped your inner child include:

- Constant abuse by a parent
- Not being allowed to have an opinion
- Your parents, siblings, or other family members constantly shame you
- Your boundaries were constantly violated
- You weren't allowed to be different, and you were even punished for it
- Every time you spoke up, you were yelled at or punished
- Your parents never hugged you or showed you affection
- Your family never allowed you to express your feelings, whether they were positive (like joy) or negative (like anger)
- Your parents made you feel responsible for their happiness
- Your parents didn't allow you to be a child and to play or just have fun

How Your Inner Child Impacts Your Adult Life

Every once in a while, your wounded inner child will take over and start acting out. Your wounded soul is suffering, which can show up as emotional tantrums, outrageous behaviors, or challenges whenever someone tries to get close to you. You also develop certain personality traits as a result of your inner child being stuck in the past.

Serious Trust Issues

This can result from a parent manipulating you or lying to you as a child. You think anyone you let in will hurt you or let you down.

Anxiety

You are always anxious around new situations like going to a new place, meeting new people, or having new experiences. This is mainly because you are uncomfortable with anything or anyone you aren't familiar with and can't predict what will happen or how they will act.

Guilt and Low Self-Esteem

Growing up with parents who blamed you for everything - even things that weren't your fault - can make you feel guilty. Therefore, you grow up as someone who feels like everything is their fault and suffers from unnecessary guilt. When you grow up believing you are always at fault, this can affect your self-esteem, and you never explore your talents or abilities or become aware of your self-worth.

Inability to Set Healthy Boundaries

Saying no and standing up for yourself are examples of setting healthy boundaries. However, suppose your family never respects your boundaries or accepts "no" as a full sentence. In that case, you become a people pleaser and put everyone else above yourself and your happiness.

Fear of Abandonment

You think everyone will leave you like your friends or parents (this can result from being abandoned by a parent as a child). A fear of abandonment can also lead to a fear of commitment. Even if your loved one did everything to prove they would never leave, your inner child would prevent you from believing them.

Difficulty Managing Your Emotions

As a child, you were probably neglected or abandoned by a parent. Instead of blaming them for leaving, you think it is your fault. This makes it difficult for you to manage your emotions and direct your anger to the right person.

Fear of Speaking Up

Maybe your parents judged you every time you spoke up or made you feel unheard or that your opinion didn't matter. This can also prevent you from setting healthy boundaries, and you give others a chance for others to control your life.

Addiction Tendencies

If you are addicted to drugs or alcohol, this can be your inner child trying to numb the pain instead of confronting it. Addiction is one of the most obvious and dangerous signs your inner child needs attention.

You Feel Unloved

Suppose your parents were emotionally unavailable when you were young. In that case, you grow up feeling unloved because no one showed you that you are worthy of love.

Negative Thoughts

Whenever you are upset or face a challenge like not getting a job, you start having negative and belittling thoughts about yourself, such as "I am not good enough" or "I don't have the right skills." Maybe your parents never believed in you as a child or constantly compared you to a sibling.

You Are Easily Triggered

Any situation, whether big or small, can trigger you one way or another because you remember similar situations that took place when you were a child. You spiral out of control, which can affect your well-being, relationships, and career.

You Seek Other People's Approval

If you grew up with parents who never validated you or your feelings, you would constantly seek approval elsewhere. You can't comprehend that validation comes from deep within.

Everything you do is nothing more than a defense mechanism your inner child uses to protect you from further pain.

Spiritual Growth and Mental Well-Being

How can you experience spiritual growth and improve your well-being if your inner child is running the show? The first step towards healing is understanding you're not the one in control. There is another side to your personality in your unconscious mind holding you back to protect you from getting hurt. If you ignore this part of yourself or you pretend that it doesn't exist, just like a child, it will manifest in anger outbursts and tantrums. How do you deal with an angry child? You give them attention and try to understand the source of their pain.

Now that you know your inner child is responsible for some of your negative traits or unpredictable behavior, you can begin a dialogue and start to form a relationship with it. Your inner child is trying to tell you something; it is screaming for help and trying to get your attention. Listening to your inner child will allow you to take a peek into its world and learn about its pain, sufferings, hopes, and needs. This can be achieved through various methods like mediation which we will discuss in detail in the coming chapters.

Once you begin listening to your inner child and navigate through all the trauma, pain, and anger it has been holding on to, you will understand that it requires spiritual healing. Giving your inner child attention is like peeling different layers of yourself. You will begin to learn more about this part of your personality and understand what it needs so you can provide it. You may uncover things about yourself, like repressed memories or emotions.

The more you learn about your inner child, the more you understand what it needs and how to nurture it, meet its needs, and give it the love and attention it has always sought. You will begin working on its healing until it is no longer consumed with the fear that is holding you back. Once your inner child feels safe, you will also notice a difference in yourself and every aspect of your life. You will become more confident, happier, and more comfortable in your own skin. Your inner child will become a voice to motivate you to live the life you have always wanted and experience new things instead of being a voice that prevents you from living your life out of fear.

As a result of nurturing your inner child, you will experience spiritual healing and, thus, spiritual *growth* because you ate longer stuck in the past. Your inner child is now growing and evolving with you. When your spirit heals, your well-being will thrive, and your physical and mental health will improve as well.

Each of us has an inner child trying to communicate with them. Yours is part of who you are, and it is time to give it the attention it deserves. This is the only way you can let go of the past and lead a life filled with love and positivity instead of allowing fear and trauma to take the wheel.

Chapter 2: Archetypes of the Inner Child

Archetypal patterns can be found everywhere. When we understand the importance of learning about them and begin digging deep into their meanings, we can learn a lot more about ourselves and the world around us. Have you ever seen a grown man turn into a child right before your eyes? Maybe their face suddenly lit up, and they started giggling uncontrollably when they heard their favorite song on the radio. Maybe this was the first time you've ever seen them let loose and drop their serious expression. How does this extreme shift happen?

Regardless of how old we get, a child archetype will always live within us. This archetype is born with us and is nurtured throughout our lifetime. It is the stepping stone of our entire personality, growth, and personal development. The greatest thing about the child archetype is that it's so much more than just a mental formulation of the human mind and psyche; it is also an aspect of our souls. Child archetypes are ever-lasting and never diminish, nor are they an invention of our past experiences, as opposed to popular belief.

The child archetype continues to impact our actions, behaviors, and view of life even as adults. The inner child affects our perceptions, understanding of everything around us, and interpretation of the world. The impact of the archetype is typically the most prominent when it comes to concepts of nurturing ourselves, caring for others, family, our outlook on life, loyalty, and safety. Connecting with your inner child requires you to reflect on your unmet desires during your childhood. You must also explore your unhelpful and childish behaviors, particularly those that influence your relationships' quality and your ability to make rational and calculated decisions. Think of your inner child as a child of your own. Your child archetype is your first child. You need to nurture it, care for it, parent it, and continue to raise it throughout your life journey. Nurturing your inner child is perhaps the greatest act of self-care there is. It is the best gift you can ever offer yourself.

There are two sides to the child archetype: the conscious, which is also known as the light side, and the unconscious, which is the dark or shadow side. In other words, the former represents your independence, and the latter corresponds to your dependence. The polarity of the inner child can be essentially thought of as how you handle your responsibilities, balance your duties, depend on yourself or others, and how others can depend on you. Acknowledging your inner child, exploring its needs, catering to its needs, as well as cultivating a healthy relationship with it can allow you to improve these aspects of your being. It can help you unleash your creativity, improve your relationships, heal past traumas, make better decisions, and attain independence.

In this chapter, you will learn more about the inner child archetype and how it can help you promote your spiritual well-being. You will then learn about the six archetypes, find out their attributes and signs, and understand their challenges. Finally, you will come across a quiz that can help you identify the archetype your inner child encompasses.

What Is the Inner Child Archetype?

When we say that the child archetype overtakes someone, we don't necessarily mean that they're acting childish. It's not their behavior that reflects the archetype, for the most part, but rather their repressed thoughts and conversations that go on inside their minds. Your inner child is begging to come out when you can't seem to shake the overwhelming emotions and thoughts tied to your childhood. Your child archetype, at its core, is the part of you that ensures that all your actions are aligned with the first thing it has learned, which is the construct of cause and effect.

Your inner child yearns for safety and protection. It wants a secure, perfect life. It will do everything within its power to ensure that you're protecting and nurturing it. At the same time, your child archetype is convinced that everything, whether good or bad, happens to you because you deserve it. The next time you tell yourself that you don't deserve your friend's betrayal, for instance, know that this is your inner child speaking.

Your child archetype sees life as black or white. It is not yet cognizant of the grays and blurry areas. It will only recognize events as either fair or unfair. It will only view you as either deserving or undeserving. When you expect a raise or a promotion, your inner child acknowledges your hard work and therefore believes it's only fair for you to be compensated.

Did you ever seek anyone's validation? You'd be lying if you said you didn't. Even the most confident individuals need someone to tell them that they're doing a great job from time to time. We all need someone to acknowledge our efforts and express how much they're proud of us. This is because our inner child doesn't recognize the concept 0f self-approval yet. As kids, our perceptions of ourselves were primarily set by how our parents viewed us. We waited to see if our parents would approve of our actions before we approved of ourselves. Our friends at school determined our self-worth. If we were made fun of, we immediately believed something was wrong with us. If we were part of the group, then we were on the safe side. A child, and the inner child, don't realize that we can approve of ourselves before anyone else does.

We all strive for our own self-approval. This is why it's important to realize that no matter how positive people's opinions are of us, they will never fulfill the unshakeable need to love and accept ourselves. Making a conscious effort with your inner child and embarking on the journey to self-discovery and acceptance will eventually lead you to self-approval. Only then will your need for external validation will falter. You will not reject people's approval- it's against human nature. However, you will not be bound to it.

Inner Child vs. Child Archetype

You must understand your inner child before exploring your child's archetype. The idea of the inner child was first developed in the field of healing therapy and psychology during the 1960s. As more people understood the validity and importance of this concept, its popularity grew significantly over the years. Now, it is not just a very important aspect of psychology and mental health but also a pillar of spiritual healing and well-being.

As we mentioned above, the inner child is the aspect of our psyche that is made of all we experienced and learned throughout our childhood. Working with this aspect of our spiritual and psychological being will allow you to determine the looming needs and wishes that have never been catered to in your childhood. This journey will also help you uncover immature behaviors and shadow patterns (remember the two sides of the child archetype?) that result in harmful behaviors and destructive life choices in adulthood.

On the other hand, the child archetype is not a product of what you've learned. As you can recall, it is also an element of your soul. This timeless aspect of your being is not past-oriented, even though your childhood influences a portion of it. Healing your inner child requires you to face and overcome past traumas or experiences. However, working with your child archetype encourages you to engage with this part of yourself and explore its light and dark (or shadow) ends of the spectrum.

Inner Child Healing

When we speak of the inner child, the idea that often comes up is that of healing. People who have suffered from traumatic incidents in their childhoods can benefit from healing their inner child. Understanding these parts of themselves and approaching them with compassion can help them revisit the memories that they've been repressing for years. Although it's often painful, the process is incredibly transformative. This healing process also applies to one of the child archetypes known as the wounded child.

The Child Archetype Motivations

When it comes to the child archetype, the main tension arises from the dichotomy that highlights the concepts of dependence and independence. There is constant strife between the need to belong and the desire to stand out. We want to be independent but still want to find a place among others. The health of your child archetype is what determines how you find a balance between those two ends of the spectrum. When working with this aspect of your spirit, you must reflect on your dependence and independence patterns. Are you consistently individualistic and hyper-independent or over-dependent, or are you constantly shifting between both extremities? How do you feel about relying on someone from time to time? Do you bite off more than you can chew and insist that you can juggle numerous responsibilities? Perhaps you avoid all commitments whenever you can.

Take the time to reflect on your relationships and responsibilities. Determine the things and people you are responsible for and those responsible for you. It can be very easy to say that you're responsible for yourself and no one else is. However, don't forget to factor in your boss at work, your doctor, your insurance company, your spouse, etc.; They are all responsible for you in one way or another.

Think about the level of your involvement in your community. How "present" are you in terms of your family? Do you have a family of your own? If not, is there a particular reason stopping you from building one? Do you visit your parents or relatives often? What is your relationship with them? Are you an active member of your community? These questions will teach you more about your child's archetype. Whether you go with the flow or take the initiative, standing up for your needs and desires is among the child archetype's most prominent challenges.

Whenever we're feeling overwhelmed or struggling to snap into the present moment, we must take a break from everything. Put your chores on pause, stop working or studying, and let go of the need to make any effort. Allow yourself to take a break from everything, your thoughts included. Call on your child archetype and invite it to spend time with you. Allow it to show you how to play and spend your time. Detach from all expectations and allow yourself to have fun. Discover what you love to do and drop the to-do list for the time being.

The 6 Child Archetypes

There are numerous child archetypes out there. Each archetype manifests its balance of the light and shadow spectrum. They are all associated with a range of positive and negative qualities. Even though we may reflect the traits of several archetypes throughout our lifetimes, we are portrayed by the one that resonates the most with us.

1. The Magical (or Innocent) Child

The magical child is fascinated by everyone around them and is also an element of fascination for others. They manage to find the silver lining in all situations and trust in the innate goodness of others. Innocent child maintains their strength, wisdom, and courage even in times of disaster. They believe that anything is possible and that all can change for the better. They are carefree and enchanted by the world around them. This archetype is the epitome of a dreamer.

However, their shadow side is that they can easily become cynical, even about the things they used to fantasize about for hours on end. They can go from believing in magic and fairy tales to destroying the dreams of others. The magic child's dark side can lead to depression, and their main challenge is that they can resort to fantasy worlds to escape reality. This may be your child archetype if you struggle with TV, books, substance, or video game addictions. When unbalanced, they lose touch with reality. An innocent child often refuses to take the initiative, which causes them to push people away. Instead of pulling themselves out of a rut, they wait for someone to come along and do it for them.

2. The Orphan Child

The orphan child archetype feels like they don't belong. They are not necessarily orphaned but spiritually, emotionally, or even physically abandoned. Their parents or loved ones may have never catered to this archetype's physical and emotional needs. If you're an orphan child, then chances are you struggle to build strong and healthy relationships with your family. You may also struggle with intense feelings of loneliness.

The orphan child may end up making it their mission to become completely independent on their life journey. They are adamant about learning things on their own, overcoming their fears all by themselves, and avoiding groups of people. The only person they trust is themselves. While independence and the keenness on self-growth and development is an upside, this archetype has a strong shadow aspect. The orphan child archetype incessantly pushes everyone away. They isolate themselves and don't allow anyone in. They compensate for this loneliness and feelings of being unwanted by searching for family in alternative places. Their main challenge is the struggle to find balance when it comes to cultivating and maintaining relationships with others. They need to learn to trust.

3. The Wounded Child

As you can infer from the name, the wounded child carries a great deal of trauma and painful experiences from their childhood. Neglect, abuse, and other impactful situations inevitably influence this archetype's relationships, decisions, and coping mechanisms. The wounded child often feels immense anger and resentment toward their caretakers. In most cases, these individuals will take it upon themselves to aid others who have gone through similar experiences. Your wounded child may come into play to protect you if you've ever encountered trauma as a kid.

This archetype usually endures abusive relationships because their shadow side keeps them stuck in a self-victimizing cycle. They can't help but grieve their situation and pity themselves. They're quick to blame everyone around them for how they are and are always going about how horrible things have turned out for them. The wounded child struggles to overcome negative emotions. They feel like no one understands.

On the other hand, their empathy urges them to jump in at the first opportunity to help others, especially those stuck in patronizing relationships. When balanced, the wounded child archetype is compassionate and forgiving. They can be the reason why someone feels understood. They can even serve as a source of strength for those who need to heal.

The main challenge for this archetype is that they may allow their childhood wounds to impact their adulthood and may struggle to find healthy ways to deal with the trauma.

4. The Nature Child

The nature child cultivates deep connections with everything in nature. They can form indispensable bonds with animals and easily communicate with them. They are rooted in the earth and are drawn to animal spirit guides. While they are clearly empathetic, emotional, and sympathetic, these individuals are also strong and resilient.

When balanced, the natural child archetype loves to connect with the earth. They love to breathe in the crisp air, walk barefoot on sandy beaches, and observe the various hues of nature. However, their shadow side may cause them to take their anger out on everything around them. They may abuse people, animals, plants, and nature. Instead of enjoying nature, they take out their negative emotions on it. They may litter, cut down plants, or express unreasonable hatred toward animals.

5. The Eternal Child

The eternal child wants to stay physically, mentally, and spiritually young. This causes them to avoid responsibilities and commitments. These individuals are on a mission to live life to the fullest. They are characterized by their optimistic, bright, and almost innocent outlook on life.

However, these individuals are very resistant when it comes to taking on adult responsibilities. They are very unreliable and often overstep the boundaries of others. The main challenge here is the struggle to accept that aging is an unavoidable aspect of life. They need to acknowledge their responsibilities and find a balance between staying youthful and leaning into adulthood.

6. The Divine Child

The divine child and the magical child archetypes are very similar. However, the divine child archetype is on a rather prophetic mission. These individuals are innocent and pure, making it hard for adults with this archetype to distinguish themselves. At first glance, you may not realize that you have a divine child inside of you.

The divine child compensates for painful experiences by resorting to spiritual endeavors or places associated with joy and development. They have an inexplicable faith that things will work out for the best. They typically believe in a divine entity.

Their shadow side is characterized by a tendency to allow fear to drive their actions. In doing so, they may hurt others before they are hurt.

Quiz: What Inner Child Archetype Am I?

Answer the following yes or no questions in the "answers" section below. The archetype with the highest number of yes answers is the archetype you belong to.

1. I generally feel safe.
2. I was often neglected as a child.
3. I feel misunderstood by other people.
4. I feel at home when I spend time in nature.
5. I run away from responsibilities.
6. I'm always excited about what's to come next.
7. I truly believe that no one intends to hurt another person.
8. Life is a constant series of heartaches.
9. Changes in the world around me scare me.
10. I feel attuned to the natural cycles of the world.
11. I am struggling to find the right job for my needs.
12. I am open to experiencing the adventures of life.
13. I trust that others will take care of me.
14. I am afraid of those in authoritarian positions.
15. I struggle with self-worth and self-esteem.
16. I am afraid of not surviving.
17. I am sometimes overtaken by a false sense of arrogance.
18. I usually find myself the center of attention.
19. I believe that the world is a safe place to be.
20. I feel abandoned.
21. I feel anxious when my sense of security is slightly shaken.
22. I often worry about being betrayed.
23. I try my best to live my life to the fullest, regardless of the consequences.

24. I have faith that things will work out for the best, even when it doesn't seem like it at times.

Answers:

The Innocent Child:

1:

7:

13:

19:

The Orphan Child:

2:

8:

14:

20:

The Wounded Child:

3:

9:

15:

21:

The Nature Child:

4:

10:

16:

22:

The Eternal Child:

5:

11:

17:

23:

The Divine Child:

6:

12:

18:

24:

No matter how hard we try to fight it, our inner child survives within us, demanding its rights. It is an active part of who we are, asking for attention and requiring acknowledgment. The child archetype wishes to be heard. It is where our random playful outbursts, moments of innocence, creativity, and wild imagination come from. While it never goes away, the inner child's voice becomes quieter as we go into our teenage years. With the pressures and expectations that come with adulthood, we often feel the urge to repress the inner child. As this voice grows less prominent, we think we've successfully overcome it, and we think that we can put it behind us forever. However, this is never the case.

Chapter 3: Discovering Your Inner Child

If you don't go back to save your inner child, who will? You are the only one who can connect with it and understand what it is going through. As we grow older, we lose touch with our inner child. We forget about this innocent part of ourselves that still experiences child-like emotions and needs mothering. We neglect our hopes, dreams, and needs and become only concerned with what our adult self wants. Your inner child is also the part that holds on to your pain and trauma, which can impact your decisions and reactions. No one can deny its role in shaping our personality, which begs the question, why don't we pay attention to it?

There is always a hidden reason or a trigger behind our unpredictable actions or reactions. Your inner child is a part of your subconsciousness, holding the answer to the question, "why am I like this?" If you don't acknowledge this side of your personality, you may never fully understand who you are or why you experience certain emotions.

You need to reflect to discover your inner child.
https://unsplash.com/photos/bbjmFMdWYfw

Finding your inner child is vital to your healing. Your wounded soul requires tending to - so you can move on from all the trauma you have experienced through the years. However, how can you fix a problem if you aren't conscious of it? How can you meet your inner child's needs when you don't know what these needs are? Healing requires you to go on a journey of self-discovery and to come face to face with your trauma, pain, and fears. Simply put, to heal, you must confront your inner child to get to the root of your trauma. If you are unconscious of your inner child, it will take over when you least expect it and overpower you.

Discovering your inner child, as the name suggests, is becoming conscious of your wounded soul, recognizing it, acknowledging its existence, and giving it the love and compassion it has always needed. This journey of self-discovery will allow you to embrace and accept your inner child as a part of who you are rather than fighting it, ignoring it, or numbing the pain. That said, you can't go on this journey without first learning to love and value yourself. Believing in yourself, your abilities, and your skills will motivate you to not only discover yourself but also believe that you have it in you to heal your wounds.

As you begin to discover and embrace your wounded soul, you will see this part of yourself as a helpless little child needing love, compassion, and acceptance. Although finding your inner child is greatly beneficial to your wellbeing, it can be a big and terrifying step for some people. You don't know what you will uncover on this journey. Your inner child can be happy and healthy or traumatized by things you may not even remember.

Benefits of Discovering Your Inner Child

Uncovering your inner child will help you release the pain and trauma that wounded your soul. When your inner child is healed, you begin navigating life as an adult who makes decisions and faces challenges instead of being just scared. Our inner child has needs, but every time it communicates them to us, we dismiss them as unnecessary. Needs like love, security, boundaries, spontaneity, and validation are valid needs. If they aren't met, this can affect our mental health. Because of this, you should find your inner child, listen to it, nurture it, and meet its needs to lead a fulfilled and happy life.

There are many benefits to discovering your inner child and connecting with it. Your inner child is trying to reach out to you, and it has been trying to get your attention. So, answer the call, get in touch with this part of yourself, and notice how various areas of your life will improve.

Boosting Your Self-Confidence

Once you get in touch with your inner child, you will begin your journey toward self-healing. Accessing this part of yourself will awaken the playful side of your inner child, who loves to have fun, try new things, and go on adventures. As a result, you will become bolder, more confident, and more determined to achieve your goals. You will have a mentality of "if I can discover my inner child and work on it, I can do anything."

Self-Care

Getting to know your inner child is a form of self-care in itself. It will give you a chance to learn about its needs so you can work on fulfilling them and thus take care of yourself and your wellbeing. Your wounded soul will feel like a real child that you have to care for and protect, like a mother who won't let anyone hurt her baby. Therefore, you will make self-care a priority.

Feeling Playful

As you gain access to your inner child, you learn about the pain, trauma, and fun and child-like aspects of your personality. You free yourself from all the constraints of adulthood, let go, and have fun. You experience a feeling of relaxation away from the seriousness and responsibilities of adulthood, even if it is just for a short while. This can do wonders for your physical and mental health.

Understanding Yourself

Discovering your inner child will reacquaint you with yourself. You will find out things about your past or your personality that you have either forgotten about or repressed, like certain emotions and memories. Through this self-discovery, you can find the source of your pain affecting your actions and decisions as an adult so you can take the necessary steps to work on yourself.

Improving Your Physical Health

Many people aren't aware of the benefits of understanding and getting to know themselves better. Self-awareness helps you relate to others and feel connected to the world around you, making you feel that you belong somewhere. A sense of belonging and community can boost your immune system and improve your physical health.

Self-Love

Self-love is often confused with narcissism or ego; however, it can't be more different. Many people are reluctant to love themselves and consider the whole notion to be strange. Getting in touch with your inner child will make you see yourself in a different light. You get acquainted with this innocent and vulnerable part of yourself that needs to be loved. You will sympathize with it and provide it with the love and compassion it has always yearned for. Once you accept your inner child as a part of who you are, you will experience true self-love.

Symptoms of Discovering Your Inner Child

As you begin your journey of self-discovery, you should be prepared for anything. By accessing this part of your personality, you will experience a wide range of emotions; some are positive, while others are negative. Take advantage of all the positive emotions and let them be a force that drives you to heal, grow, and enjoy life. Negative emotions will give you an idea of the wounds and trauma you have been suffering from all this time so you can work through your issues and finally heal.

Positive Emotions

- Creativity
- Joy
- Playfulness
- A desire to have fun
- A light-hearted attitude
- Feeling less emotionally numb and disconnected

Negative Emotions

- Becoming aware of repressed memories and emotions
- Childhood trauma
- Pain and fear

Challenges of Discovering Your Wounded Soul

Don't expect this journey of self-discovery to be a smooth ride; there will be some challenges along the way you should be prepared for. Connecting with your inner child can be triggering if you have suffered from traumatic experiences during your childhood. You will find yourself being confronted with repressed memories and emotions that you aren't ready to revisit. Remembering things you have fought hard to forget or repress may discourage you from continuing on this journey. It can be challenging to face these memories, so you would rather ignore your inner child than try to uncover your trauma. You may also be ashamed of having a scared and vulnerable inner child. However, you aren't alone; each one of us has an inner child. The only difference is some are happy and satisfied while others are traumatized and struggling.

Many people face these challenges, and it is pretty normal. The pain and fear they experience after being exposed to emotions and memories they have long tried to avoid can be emotionally and mentally draining. As a result, they quit, leaving their inner child wounded and numbing the pain with unhealthy coping mechanisms like alcohol or drugs.

No one said healing is easy, but it is worth it. Learning there is a part of you that is traumatized can be both shocking and hard to deal with. However, you should let this pain motivate you to take your inner child by the hand and help it move on and grow. Once it does, you can be free from past pain. It is a long, hard road that begins with one vital step: discovering your wounded soul.

A Guide to Discovering Your Inner Child

In this part of the chapter, we will provide you with a simple guide to help you uncover your inner wounded soul. Reaching out to your inner child isn't easy. It has its challenges and may take a while. You shouldn't fret or give in; eventually, you will get there and uncover its secrets.

Open Your Mind

Before you embark on your journey of self-discovery, you should first open yourself up to the idea of an inner child. Having doubts at first is normal, but you should regard your inner child as a part of you, not as something separate. Simply put, change your perspective. You aren't discovering your "inner child" per se, but you are discovering your past relationships and experiences. Not believing in the idea of an inner child or that you can connect with it can create a barrier that prevents you from uncovering it.

Daydream

Sit alone in a quiet room, close your eyes, and allow your mind to travel back to your childhood. Think of how simple things were back then with no responsibilities, running free, and being spontaneous and silly. You didn't care about money; the simplest things made you happy. You laughed until your stomach hurt, and the word "stress" didn't even have meaning to you. Now, open your eyes and write down everything you saw and felt. Did these thoughts evoke happy and joyful emotions? Or was your childhood so traumatic that it evoked pain and fear? Write it all down, including what specifically made you happy as a child and what caused you the most pain and suffering.

Do Things You Enjoyed as a Child

Treat your inner child as someone you want to get to know. Try to find what they like so you can connect with them and get close to them. So how can you learn about your inner child's hobbies? Simply think of the things you used to enjoy as a child-like riding your bicycle, swimming in the pool with your best friends, going roller skating, dancing, or spending the day at the library. Whatever you did as a child, you did it for one purpose only: to have fun. You didn't have responsibilities and did things because you wanted to, not because you had to.

Do things you enjoyed as a child.

https://www.pexels.com/photo/photograph-of-two-girls-on-a-swing-1814433/

When was the last time you did anything just for fun? This is the perfect time to do something that used to make you happy. Go back to the time when life was simple with no stress, and your only concern was having fun. Try something creative like coloring, doodling, painting, or playing your favorite video game from your childhood. These activities will relax you, shut down your mind, and awaken emotions you may have forgotten about. Some of these emotions or memories can manifest in your drawings or doodling.

Seek the Help of a Child

As an adult, you may struggle to see things from a child's perspective. Many of us have forgotten how to have a child-like attitude. Seeking the help of a child, like your son, daughter, nieces, or nephews, can be very helpful. In fact, there are many things we can learn from children. Spend some time with any children in your family and play fun games like hide-and-seek or tag. These games will help you let go of the constraints of adulthood as you run around feeling free and having fun. Watching your favorite cartoon as a child or reading your favorite childhood book can bring back positive memories and emotions as well.

You can also try playing make-believe scenarios like pretending you are Darth Vader and running around chasing the kids. Make-believe scenarios can take you back to your childhood fantasies and dreams. However, this game may not always awaken heart-warming emotions and memories. If you experienced trauma as a child and used your imagination as a coping mechanism to escape your harsh reality, you may find yourself remembering these moments.

Start a Dialogue with Your Inner Child

Having a conversation with someone can teach us so much about them. The same can be applied to your inner child as well. We aren't saying you should start talking to yourself (however, if it can help, do it), but you can talk to your inner child through journaling. For instance, if you experienced a traumatic event as a child, writing about it can help you get in touch with your inner child. You can write a letter to yourself or explore some of your memories and write about them in your diary. While writing, think of a specific memory and write everything that comes to mind, don't hold back. You can also do a Q&A by asking your inner child questions and writing down the answers. Acknowledging your inner child at this very moment, embracing the idea without any doubts, and listening to what it is trying to tell you are all crucial for this step to work.

Look inward, self-reflect, and try to access all your buried emotions and memories so you can communicate with your wounded soul. You will not only learn so much about your inner child through writing, but you will also establish a bond with it as well.

Take a Trip Down Memory Lane

Your inner child is still stuck in the past, so you should take a trip back in time to connect with it. You can relive memories in various ways, like looking at old pictures, reading your childhood diary, or looking at your childhood stuff like your toys. Scents are also known to help conjure memories, so try smelling an old perfume or deodorant. For instance, if you catch the scent of your favorite dish, you will remember all the times your grandma made it and all the sweet memories you shared. You can also ask your childhood friends, siblings, parents, or other family members to share stories from your childhood with you. These stories may evoke sweet, bittersweet, or painful memories and emotions.

Seek the Help of a Therapist

This process isn't easy, and you may encounter some challenges along the way. In some cases, trying to uncover your inner child may trigger painful memories and emotions. For this reason, seeking the help of a professional can be what you need to find your inner child. A therapist will walk you through the process of discovering your wounded soul and provide advice and guidance to help you cope with traumatic memories. They can also help you uncover repressed memories and emotions that you buried deep because you don't want to face them. Make sure to find a therapist who has experience in inner child work.

Quiz

We recommend you work on the steps mentioned above for some time first before taking this quiz.

Have I Discovered My Inner Child?

We will provide you with a list of yes or no questions, and your answers will determine if you have discovered your inner child or not. Think hard and take your time with each question.

1. Do you feel more creative than before?
   - o Yes
   - o No
2. Do you feel more playful and feel like you want to have fun?
   - o Yes
   - o No
3. Do you feel more in touch with child-like emotions like joy and a carefree attitude or anger and throwing tantrums?
   - o Yes
   - o No

4. Do you feel the desire to practice an old childhood activity or play an old childhood game?
    - Yes
    - No
5. Do you feel less emotionally numb than before?
    - Yes
    - No
6. Have you recently uncovered a childhood trauma or a painful memory you haven't thought of in years?
    - Yes
    - No
7. Have repressed emotions begun to resurface?
    - Yes
    - No
8. Do pictures or certain scents bring back memories from your childhood (good or bad)?
    - Yes
    - No
9. Do you often daydream about your childhood?
    - Yes
    - No
10. Do you enjoy spending time with children?
    - Yes
    - No
11. Does journaling help you uncover things about yourself?
    - Yes
    - No

Ideally, you should answer "yes" to all or most of these questions. However, if most of your answers are "no," then you still need to work on yourself to discover your inner child.

Don't feel discouraged if you haven't uncovered your wounded soul yet. This is a long process, and it will take time and effort to get there. It can also be a traumatic experience for some people, which can prolong the process.

The road to healing begins with one single step, and this step is discovering your inner child so you can connect with it. It is a road that may be filled with challenges for some people. Your inner child needs you and has been calling out for you through certain child-like actions and emotions. You have been ignoring it for long enough. It is time to act now and give it the attention it needs.

Discovering your inner child will help you learn about yourself and eventually accept the fact that it is a part of who you are. Your wounded soul is a part of your journey, an important chapter in your story that you can't simply ignore or skip.

Chapter 4: Accepting Your Inner Child

"Yes, I feel you, I know you are here, and I accept you."

We all want to be loved, embraced, and accepted for who we are. Our inner child is no different; it yearns for acceptance too. No one can deny the importance of self-acceptance and its role in boosting our self-esteem and leading a healthy and fulfilled life. We all want to be happy; it is the goal most of us chase and has in common. Accepting your inner child will reconnect you with the part of yourself you have been ignoring for so long. You will learn about it, understand its pain, and eventually grow to love it and accept it. Everything you experienced as a child - even the trauma - is part of you and impacts shaping the person you have become. Fighting your pain will only give it power. However, once you accept it as a part of your journey, you take its power away and begin to see your inner child as someone vulnerable, scared, and who just wants to be embraced.

It's important to embrace your inner child.

https://www.pexels.com/photo/a-woman-in-knit-sweater-hugging-self-5709914/

As adults, people usually think they have figured everything out about themselves and the world around them. What if we told you that you not only don't have everything figured out, but you also need to unlearn some of the habits you have picked up over the years? Embracing your inner child is your chance to unlearn all the bad habits and personality traits that resulted from your trauma.

By growing up deprived of love and believing you aren't good enough, your inner child begins seeking perfection and makes you believe that if you aren't perfect, you aren't worthy of love. Perfection is an illusion; the more you chase it, the more frustrated you will be. Eventually, you will despise this part of yourself. However, when you listen, accept, and nurture your inner child, you will understand that it only wants to protect you. Therefore, you stop resenting it and begin to love and sympathize with this vulnerable inner child that doesn't know any better.

Accepting your inner child is just as the name suggests; you fully accept your inner child as part of your past, present, and future and its role in shaping your adult personality. You accept it without judgment or shame and embrace it with all its trauma and pain. Acceptance is the most valuable gift you can give anyone so imagine doing the same for yourself. It is another vital step you should be taking towards healing your inner child and moving on from the past to a brighter and happier future.

That said, you won't be able to accept your inner child before it is fully and truly discovered. How can you accept something you can't find? As mentioned in the previous chapter, discovering your inner child is the first step you should take before you begin your healing. Once you find it and understand that its pain, fear, joy, and trauma are part of who you are, you can begin accepting and embracing it. Your inner child is you; this is a fact you should never deny, fight, or be ashamed of.

The Importance of Accepting Your Wounded Soul

If you are struggling to accept your wounded soul, how will you be able to heal? You can't live your life fighting with a part of yourself or living in shame of it. Acknowledge it and accept it so you can grow stronger and let go of the past. Accepting your wounded soul can help you become a happier and more forgiving person, not just to yourself but to others as well.

Deep inside you lies all the answers you seek. All you need to do is self-reflect, and you will find what you are looking for. You can't keep ignoring your wounded soul. It has been sending you messages all your life through your anxiety, self-criticism, and even depression. Once you fully accept your inner child, you can finally understand the meaning behind these messages. There is a reason behind your anxieties, there is a reason why you want to please people and struggle with saying no, and there is a reason why you have had relationship issues all your life. Your traumatic childhood is the reason behind many of the issues you have in your adult life. Embracing your inner child means you understand that it can be the root cause of many of the problems you have now. You are willing to look for solutions to help yourself instead of silencing or rejecting them.

Accepting your wounded soul means you are ready to heal and are taking the necessary steps to help yourself recover from your past experiences. Your inner child is a sensitive and innocent soul; embracing it means tapping into its positive side with all its wonderful qualities as well. It will remind you to love, forgive, and be honest with yourself and the world around you.

Forgiveness

Kids don't hold grudges. Remember when you were a kid and fought with your best friend or siblings? Did you hold grudges? Kids get over fighting quickly and go back to playing with each other as if nothing happened. When you embrace your inner child, you embrace every part of it, including the ability to forgive. Accepting your inner child will help you see that you are a victim of a bad childhood or bad circumstances. As a result, you will learn to be kinder to yourself and to forgive yourself for any mistakes you have made when your wounded soul takes over.

Honesty

Who is more honest than a child? At times, they can be brutally honest. They speak their mind with no fear of judgment. Unlike us, they don't tiptoe around the truth. When was the last time you spoke your mind without worrying if others would judge you? Do you sometimes hold back from telling the truth? Embracing your inner child will help you approach your relationships and life with an honest attitude. Understanding and accepting that a part of you is damaged will open your eyes and encourage you to be more honest with yourself about your struggles and understand that healing is more of a necessity than an option.

How to Accept Your Inner Child

Now, let's discuss methods to help you accept your wounded soul. We can't stress the importance of embracing this part of yourself enough. In fact, it is an essential step in your healing process.

1. Mother Your Inner Child

Every child needs a mother to nurture and care for them. Embrace your inner child by giving it the motherly love and affection it has always craved. Not every child grows up in a loving home with caring parents. There are narcissistic or immature parents who are unable to love their children. Even the best parents had moments when they were too busy, lost their temper, or yelled at their kids. They never meant to hurt their children, but they are still humans who make mistakes sometimes. However, a child doesn't see it this way, and these things can last with them forever.

As an adult who wasn't loved or is still reeling from certain childhood issues, you are always hard on yourself whenever you make a mistake. You become self-critical, feel guilty, or belittle yourself. Imagine if you treated a child the same way every time they made a mistake. Can you look an innocent child in the eye and belittle them if they do something wrong? How will this affect their mental health and wellbeing? Your inner child, as mentioned, is the child-like part of you, and you should treat it as such. To accept and embrace it, watch your thoughts every time you make a mistake. Instead of the negativity, mother and nurture your inner child by comforting it. Your wounded soul is scared and needs reassurance. Being kind and loving to this vulnerable part of yourself is how you prove that you have fully accepted it.

2. Achieve Your Inner Child Dreams

Think of a dream you wanted to achieve when you grow up. There are no limits to a child's imagination; they believe they can do anything and achieve anything. However, as we grow up, we start having more realistic or practical dreams. Some people in our lives will always discourage us from following our dreams and tell us to look for more steady careers. We forget about these dreams with age, but our inner child still remembers each one we have ever had.

To fully accept this part of your personality, you can achieve one or more of your childhood dreams. We aren't saying you should quit your job or leave your responsibilities behind. You can still achieve your dream without jeopardizing your career. For instance, if you have always wanted to be an artist, you can take an art class, or if you have wanted to be a writer, you can take a creative writing class. Believe in yourself and show your inner child that you still believe anything is possible.

3. Play Games or Dance

We have mentioned in the previous chapter how playing with children, doing something creative you enjoyed as a child, or just dancing can help you discover your inner child. These fun childhood activities can also help you accept your wounded soul. Doing things your inner child enjoys is a great way to show it and to show yourself that you accept and embrace this part of yourself. So, draw, paint, play games, play some music, and dance like no one is watching, or go to karaoke with your friends and sing your heart out. Even if you have a bad voice, don't be afraid of making a fool out of yourself.

4. Listen to Your Inner Child

How can you accept your wounded soul if you aren't actively listening to it? We have talked before about how your inner child communicates with you through strong emotions resulting from triggering situations. Instead of dismissing these emotions, take a closer look at them to understand why you were even triggered in the first place.

For instance, you and your best friend were supposed to meet but canceled at the last minute. Instead of understanding that we all have responsibilities and things can come up, you feel rejected. You act like a child and refuse to answer your friend's calls or messages. When you cool down and see your friend's messages, you realize that their partner had an accident which is why they had to cancel on you. Now you feel terrible for reacting like a "child" and frustrated and angry with yourself.

This tantrum is your wounded soul communicating its pain to you. To show your inner child acceptance, listen to what it is trying to tell you. Understand why it acted this way. Why did you feel rejected when your friend canceled? Maybe your parents were always busy and had to cancel plans or never showed up for your football games or ballet recitals. Listening to your inner child's emotions and seeing the situation from their perspective is a great step toward accepting this part of yourself rather than feeling guilty or rejecting these feelings.

5. Identify Your Inner Child

In a previous chapter, we discussed the archetypes of the inner child and how you can identify yours. Identifying your inner child will help you accept it for what it is without trying to change it.

6. Take Your Inner Child Seriously

You may think whatever your inner child feels is irrelevant to you. Throwing tantrums, feeling rejected, or wanting to play may seem like childish needs to an adult. So instead of paying attention to them, you end up ignoring them. However, there is always a reason behind all your childhood needs, and it comes from something deeper. So, take your inner child seriously and meet its needs.

7. Be Kind to Your Inner Child

Your inner child is hurt, broken, scared, and looking for acceptance. Most wounded souls just want to know they are cared for. No one but you can save your inner child. Remind your hurt and broken soul every once in a while that you love it. Whenever you look in the mirror, say "I love you" to yourself.

If you had a traumatic childhood or were abused or abandoned, your inner child probably believes it was their fault. Now, as you have grown up and realized that none of it was your fault, let your inner child know this as well. Tell it that you didn't deserve this childhood; you deserved to be loved and taken care of.

Apologize to your inner child for how you acted like a child. Whether you were hard on yourself, self-critical, or put yourself last, all these things that you still do to this day are hurting your inner child. Tell your wounded soul you are sorry and protect it from further pain.

We have mentioned in previous chapters that your inner child is driven by fear, and it only wants to protect you. Even though it held you back and stored painful memories, you should still thank it for being there for you and trying to shield you from more pain. Let it know that you aren't judging it and want to thank it for trying.

Accepting your inner child isn't just saying, "I accept you." It is telling it everything it needs to hear so it can heal.

8. Protect Your Inner Child

We have mentioned above how you should treat your inner child like a mother who will protect her baby and won't let anyone hurt it. Your inner child is your baby, and part of accepting it is constantly acknowledging its existence. This is done by checking on it to ensure it is well and keeping it away from harmful situations. Your inner child hasn't healed yet, so show it kindness by respecting its needs. Understandably, you want to let go of your fears and not be held back by them. However, your inner child may have certain insecurities or fears, so treat them more sensitively. For instance, avoid places like elevators if you fear closed spaces - something that began in your childhood. If you have a toxic friend or family member that increases your anxiety, avoid them as much as you can and limit communication with them. Protect your inner child as you protect your real child or your pet.

Accepting Your Inner Child and Spiritual Growth

Accepting your inner child is a process of spiritual growth. It is a long road that will take time and effort. This process isn't just saying to yourself, "I accept my inner child," and then moving on. You must work on embracing and accepting this part of yourself daily. It is the only way you can experience spiritual growth and healing. Take your time with this process and listen to your wounded soul's needs, take these needs seriously, and fiercely protect it just like a mother would.

As mentioned, accepting your inner child is the most important step toward healing. Through it, you will experience real growth. Let your inner child know that you accept it and will no longer ignore it, silence it, or fight it. This is the biggest decision you will make to help accelerate your healing. You aren't only acknowledging your inner child but fully accepting, embracing it, and treating it with the compassion it deserves. You understand that when your inner child heals, you will also heal and experience spiritual growth.

Quiz

Have you fully accepted your inner child? Take this quiz to find out.

1. Have you acknowledged your inner child?
   - Yes
   - No
2. Have you made your peace with the idea of having a traumatized inner child?
   - Yes
   - No
3. Do you feel proud of your inner child for putting up with so much?
   - Yes
   - No
4. Do you love your inner child?
   - Yes
   - No

5. Do you feel grateful for all that your inner child did to protect you?
    - Yes
    - No
6. Do you believe your traumatic childhood was out of your control and not your fault?
    - Yes
    - No
7. Do you feel the need to apologize to your inner child for everything it had to endure?
    - Yes
    - No
8. Do you believe your inner child deserved a better childhood?
    - Yes
    - No
9. Do you take your inner child's needs seriously?
    - Yes
    - No
10. Do you play games or do other fun activities from your childhood?
    - Yes
    - No
11. Are you aware of your inner child's archetype?
    - Yes
    - No
12. Have you tried achieving any of your childhood dreams recently?
    - Yes
    - No
13. Do you believe you have an inner child?
    - Yes
    - No

14. Do you believe your inner child is a part of you and needs healing?
    - Yes
    - No
15. Do you accept having a traumatized inner child?
    - Yes
    - No

If you answer most of these questions with "yes," then you have fully accepted your inner child. However, if you mostly answer with "no," you still need time and effort, but you will get there.

Accepting your inner child is your way of telling your past "no more." You are now taking control of your trauma, and instead of letting it defeat you, you will work on yourself to defeat it and begin your healing journey. Remember, you aren't just healing from your past but also protecting yourself from current or future trauma. Accept your inner child, love it, take care of it, and protect it from pain. When it is healed, it will be the one taking care of you and helping you grow.

Chapter 5: Inner Child Meditation

When you follow the tips from the previous chapters, successfully uncover your inner child, and accept them for who they are, you will see that they have a lot to say. However, having them buried for so long, you may not be able to communicate with your inner child right after acknowledging their existence. This chapter is dedicated to one of the simplest techniques that can help you establish a meaningful connection with your inner self - meditation. You will learn about the impact that practicing meditation has on healing the wounded soul and keeping your mental, spiritual, and physical health in check. After all, these three areas of your life are essential for your inner child's health and happiness - and meditation can help improve all of them. You will also be provided with a beginner-friendly meditation technique you can practice anytime you need to communicate with your inner child or heal yourself.

Meditation plays an important role in healing your inner child.
https://pixabay.com/es/photos/yoga-mujer-lago-al-aire-libre-2176668/

Meditation for Healing a Wounded Soul

The first step in healing your inner child and your soul from within is listening to what they say. This can be challenging as you may have trouble interpreting their messages or simply because you don't like what they are trying to say. The feelings your inner child may convey can trigger powerful emotions and discomfort, which you will only be able to process with the right tools. Not only that, but hurtful feelings such as anger, insecurity, vulnerability, anxiety, guilt, shame, or the feeling of abandonment and rejection can often be traced back to specific memories from your own childhood. Your inner child's feelings are just the reflection of these events - but their discomfort often triggers negative responses in your current life. Meditation is an immersive exercise. It lets you dive deep into the depths of your soul and reveal the origins of the negative thought processes you have in the present time. The root of your spiritual imbalance lies in your inner child's inability to process pain and hurt from the past - and meditative practice can help you move on from these traumatic experiences. To understand how this can be done, you must learn what meditation is and how it works in the first place.

What Is Meditation?

Meditation typically encompasses a range of techniques designed to help you look beyond your conscious thoughts and emotions and uncover what lies within your unconscious mind. By simply focusing your mind into its depths, meditation encourages forming a powerful connection with your inner self, allowing you to experience life more profoundly. Meditation often includes training your mind and body to stay grounded and open to anything you may experience in the present moment.

Meditation and Mindfulness

While meditation is also considered a form of mindfulness, not all mindfulness exercises are as reflective as meditation. Mindfulness brings you to the present - which is the first step in connecting with your inner child and healing them. Whereas meditation is necessary to surpass your conscious mental processes and truly see what the child within you is experiencing. Consequently, if you want to heal your inner child, you must combine these two practices.

Fortunately, mindful meditation is one of the simplest forms of meditation. You can perform it anytime, anywhere. You only need to find a place where you can focus on your thoughts, feelings, and actions as you experience them in the present. You must avoid letting the past or future color your perception, and you shouldn't allow any judgment or preconception to influence you during the process. A mindful meditation focused on healing you from the inside brings your inner child into focus by relaxing your body and allowing your mind to create a specific mental image. Since you have to focus on visualizing the child representing your deepest emotions, you are forced to remain in the present.

Benefits of Meditation for Healing Wounded Souls

As established earlier in this book, your inner child is the reflection of your soul - a reflection that is full of joy and happiness in its natural state. Any negativity your inner child experiences represents your inability to process emotional trauma. Meditation can help you restore the blissful state of your soul by making you aware of all the hurt inside of it. When you are unaware of your soul, you can only focus on your body and mind and the pain inside. However, spiritual imbalances often manifest as physical and mental symptoms, including pain and cognitive issues. By only eliminating the proximate cause of the symptoms, you are only diminishing them- but their true source remains and will eventually cause them to return. You can't comprehend why this is and continue to search for answers - when, in fact, the answers lie right there, within your inner child.

The different meditation exercises can achieve physical relaxation, mental clarity, spiritual connections, and emotional tranquility. All of these have a positive impact on healing your wounded soul and forming a solid bond with your inner child.

Here are the key benefits of inner child meditations:

- **Higher Spiritual Awareness:** As you are still yourself and withdraw your focus from your environment, your attention shifts to whatever you experience in your soul. This higher level of spiritual awareness allows you to find answers to even the most troubling questions. You realize that you have the gift to heal your soul and proceed to do just that during your sessions.
- **Increased Pain Tolerance:** In the beginning, relaxing your mind and body will make you aware of all the pain and discomfort you may feel. However, as you learn to put these aside, your nervous system will start to send fewer pain stimuli to your brain with each session. And since physical pain may be both the cause and the symptoms of a wounded soul, reducing it will put you in higher spirits.
- **Reduced Stress Levels:** When you relax your body and mind, your brain will lower your blood cortisol levels. This hormone causes prolonged effects of stress, including anxiety, depression, lack of sleep, deteriorated cognitive functions, and a whole range of negative emotions that affect your spirit. Eliminating it from the bloodstream means better physical, mental, and spiritual health. At the same time, the levels of the inhibitory neurotransmitter GABA (gamma-aminobutyric acid) in your nervous system increase. This

causes all the stress-inducing neurotransmitters to stop functioning, which has the same effect as reducing cortisol levels.

- **Improved Mood:** After each of your sessions, the levels of another hormone, serotonin, will also start increasing. Serotonin is often referred to as the feel-good hormone because it causes a general sense of well-being. Its effects are long-lasting and range across multiple plains of your life. This hormone encourages you to explore negative emotions by making you feel better. No matter how difficult facing them may be, you will be able to do it because you are filled with positive, encouraging emotions.
- **Instant Happiness Booster**: Mediation also promotes the production of endorphins - which, similarly to serotonin, causes a significant mood improvement. And while their euphoric effects don't last as long as the serotonin's, endorphins can give an instant boost when you need it. By receiving a large endorphin dose when communicating with your inner child, you can send them more positive emotions and heal them much sooner.
- **Higher Melatonin Levels:** Focusing your mind during the session will teach you how to eliminate distractions that hinder your body's ability to produce the hormone melatonin. You can triple your melatonin levels in just a few weeks by meditating for only a couple of minutes daily. As a result, you will have much better sleep, a robust immune system, and the ability to prevent many illnesses known to cause deep-seated spiritual trauma.
- **Elimination of Other Endocrine Causes:** Meditation balances out the levels of insulin and glucagon -the two hormones responsible for regulating blood sugar levels. By maintaining your glucose levels in a normal range, your body receives less stress, which means fewer causes for your spirits to be lower. Meditative practices can also increase your growth hormone levels. This endocrine chemical is responsible for maintaining the proper functions of virtually all the cells in your body. More of it means your ability to prevent physical and mental causes of spiritual imbalance

increases.

- **Improved Ability to Express Emotions:** Whether you are experiencing positive or negative feelings, you will be able to convey them in a healthy way just after a few sessions. When you start expressing your emotions, you will notice the positive effects of this act on your relationships. This leads to the production of mood-enhancing hormones discussed previously, enhancing their positive influence on your spiritual wellbeing.
- **Higher Level of Self-Acceptance:** By focusing on giving as much love to your inner child as possible, you are essentially learning how to love and accept yourself. Mediation is an incredible source of nourishment for your soul, an unrivaled confidence booster, and the spiritual benefits of having high confidence levels.
- **Healthier Priorities:** A higher state of awareness can help you rearrange your priorities by placing the healing of your soul at the top of your list. Meditation stimulates your prefrontal cortex- the part of your brain responsible for logical reasoning and thoughts about yourself. The practices can also improve your brain's ability to resist following others in actions, thoughts, and emotions that aren't in alignment with what your inner child feels or wants.

Inner Child Meditation

The following meditation technique is designed to help you reconnect with your inner child and heal them and yourself. It will allow you to see if the child within you is still holding on to painful memories even if they don't want to. It will also help you understand that behind this pain is a child that can show you what happiness truly is. With this exercise, you will learn how to unconditionally love your inner self, honor your deepest wishes, and invite peace into your life.

Here are the steps to do this exercise:

- Start by getting into a comfortable position. You can stand, sit, or even lie down - as long as you can relax your body and mind.

- Close your eyes, take a deep breath, exhale slowly, and repeat.
- Focus on your breathing as you continue to relax until you feel that the rhythm comes naturally.
- When you finally feel that you don't have to concentrate on your breathing anymore, take a mental pause and switch your focus to see if your body is relaxed.
- Check if your cheeks, jaw, and shoulders are relaxed and whether your arms and legs are in a natural position. All your body should feel warm and heavy, except for your stomach area, which should feel light.
- Take another pause and start visualizing your inner child. Take your time to take in their appearance, position, expressions, and demeanor.
- Now open your other senses and try hearing any sounds made by the child, taking in the scents around them, or acknowledging any other stimuli you receive.
- Imagine that the child is holding a dark bubble in one of their hands. Look closer at the dark sphere to see the memories within it.
- Do you sense fear, pain, or sadness in dark memories that appear as still or moving images? Or just floating emotions caused by rejection and disappointment?
- Try to persuade the child to tell you where those emotions come from. More likely than not, your inner child has created elaborate stories about those emotions. If you listen closely, you will notice that these stories resonate with your thoughts.
- In their tale, the child may tell you that they don't feel worthy or good enough to matter to anyone or have what they want. They may also tell you that they've been hurt and can no longer trust others.
- While all of these stories are entirely normal, if you feel that they interfere with your life, now is the time to change them. You can start doing this by taking a deep breath and feeling

how the air travels through your body to cleanse it.

- Release the emotions by exhaling deeply and, once again, reach out to the child. Embrace them with positive thoughts and feelings and hold them until you see the dark sphere dissipating in their hands.
- Even if it doesn't disappear completely, tell the child that you accept them even if they can't let go of all the hurt they're in right now. Tell them that they can come to you with any trouble thoughts or emotions they may have in the future.
- Now, take another pause, during which you should only focus on your breathing.
- After that, envision the child again, now with a bright sphere in their other hand. This bubble is filled with happy memories, love, laughter, dreams, and wishes.
- Feel the lightness of these emotions, whether they appear as a picture, a little film, or a simple feeling. Take your time to soak them in and let them fill you with happiness.
- See how happy the child is when they look at the sphere. See how bright their smile is, and let this smile take over you as well.
- Invite more happiness into your life by asking the child about their favorite game, event, or memory.
- Embrace the child again so you can start creating more happy memories and feel their love toward you. It's just as powerful as the one you show toward them.
- When you feel that you and your inner child are now in sync, let their image disappear, bring your attention back to your breathing and return your awareness to the world around you.

Tips for Inner Child Meditation

If you aren't familiar with meditation and other mindfulness techniques, you may find the experience somewhat peculiar. One of the aspects you may struggle with at the beginning of your journey is focusing your mind long enough for the exercise to start working.

Fortunately, whatever your inner child wants to say to you, they will get to it as soon as you establish the connection. So, if you haven't been able to understand their message in the first few minutes, sitting for an hour and trying to decipher what your inner child said won't help. It's better to reach out to them another time. If you are dealing with a pressing matter, you can try to reach out to your inner child later on the same day, and if your inquiry can wait, do it the day after your first attempt. The human brain simply can't focus on the same topic for hours because the effects of the beneficial hormones produced during meditation don't last that long. You can start as little as 2-3 minutes at a time and slowly increase the duration of the exercise as your ability to focus improves. With practice, you'll be able to establish an open line of communication with your inner child - and with their help, you will be able to heal yourself from the inside out.

If you want to improve your ability to communicate with your inner child, you should start by choosing the right time of the day for it. Due to the nature of the human circadian rhythm and the brain's tendency to process stimuli and events during sleep, the best time for meditation is early morning. Provided you have a restful night of sleep, meditating right after waking up means you are working with a relaxed, well-rested mind. This will allow you to focus your thoughts without the distractions of the day. Avoid having breakfast before meditation, as digestion itself can be a distraction.

Morning benefits notwithstanding, you can consult your inner child any time during the day. For example, you may find yourself unable to sleep due to troubling ideas about an event. In this case, even focusing on hidden thoughts about the subject for a few minutes at bedtime can give you the clarity you need to have a restful night.

Chapter 6: Inner Child Journaling

This chapter discusses journaling, another technique geared towards uncovering patterns in your current life that have origins in your past. You can step back in time and explore your inner child's pain through journaling. This practice can be valuable when dealing with deep-rooted traumas you can't or won't acknowledge through other methods. That said, before you start recording your emotions, thoughts, and memories in a journal, you should understand what journaling entails and the challenges and benefits of it. Besides empowering you with knowledge about inner child journaling, this chapter will also provide you with a simple journaling guide and a few pieces of advice on how to get the most out of it.

Journaling is an effective technique for healing.

https://pixabay.com/es/photos/computadora-port%c3%a1til-libro-cuero-420011/

What Is Wounded Soul Journaling?

Journaling is the process of exploring your thoughts and emotions and working your way to their effects by writing them down. Having your beliefs recorded on paper makes it easier to recall them. Once written, all you need to do is read them to analyze or remember their significance anytime you feel the need to do so. On paper, even the most confusing experiences get a clearer outlook. The ability to discover the proper perspective makes journaling a very effective coping strategy and a powerful tool for healing your inner child. Journaling through your inner child is designed to help you see every event in the way the child within you experiences them. This will enable you to understand how these experiences impact your spiritual health.

There are many forms of inner child journaling, but the most effective ones are geared toward uncovering specific memories. These typically involve visualizing yourself as a child at the age when these memories were formed. If you aren't sure when the painful memories were created, you should ask your inner child about them first. And when you have the answer to this question, you can move on to the exploration phase.

The Impact of Journaling on Healing Your Inner Child

If you aren't used to expressing your thoughts verbally or on paper, you may find journaling a trying experience. Many people think of journaling as they do about most school or work assignments - another task that must be completed during the day. You may be wondering what good it does to recite your negative thoughts and feelings in your head and put them on paper.

Another challenge you face in this modern world is finding writing on paper an old-fashioned way to communicate, even if it's with your inner self. With all the digital technology around us, we have come to rely on video, voice, and other means of communication. One of the greatest appeals of journaling lies in its ability to remove all the distractions of the digital age - and dissipate the stress that comes with them.

Writing down the possible sources of your issues is only part of the inner child's journaling journey. The other part is learning how to be grateful for every spiritual gift you receive in life. As you write about what your inner child is revealing to you in your visions, you'll slowly discover that everything happens for a reason. Even your negative experiences were nothing more than lessons you can learn from. And as you contemplate the meaning of these crucial lessons, everything you've experienced will be placed in a different perspective. The pain that followed the negative experiences goes away and is replaced by hope, joy, and gratitude - much to your inner child's happiness. You are the creator of your own well-being; journaling will help you understand this. Here are some of the most precious gifts you receive when you journal for your inner child:

- **Reduced Stress Levels:** Writing about what's bothering you in your day-to-day life leads to a long-term decrease in the production levels of the stress inducing-hormone cortisol. It also stimulates the release of neurotransmitters with a similar effect and disrupts pain signals. This will result in lowered blood pressure and improved liver functions, lessening the impact of stress on your physical and mental health.
- **Managing Stress in a Healthy Way:** Even if you initially can't identify the sources or triggers for your anxiety - through journaling - you can learn how to manage your condition in a healthy way. Simply expressing your thoughts about stressful or traumatic experiences will help you avoid resorting to unhealthy distractions and addictive behavior.
- **Improved Immune Response:** When your body doesn't have to combat the effects of stress, it can focus on providing sufficient protection from pathogens. Regular journaling boosts the production of T-lymphocytes, the cells responsible for the processes involved in a healthy immune response. Your wounds will heal faster; you will rebound from colds more quickly, become more productive and acquire a better outlook on life.
- **Learning How to Appreciate Different Experiences:** By discovering what makes you happy, you will learn how to appreciate the simple things in life - as they are often the most important ones. When coming in the right direction,

even the smallest gesture or sign can lead to an enormous boost in serotonin production.

- **Improved Mood:** The ability to express your thoughts, even if you can only do it on paper, will boost the production of serotonin and endorphins, chemicals responsible for making you feel good about yourself and your abilities. It also promotes the production of the neurotransmitters responsible for counteracting signals that spread negative responses throughout your body and mind.
- **Sharper Cognitive Skills:** It's a well-known fact that regular writing and reading promote the honing of cognitive skills, such as your ability to memorize things and recall them later on. By producing inhibitory neurotransmitters and feel-good hormones, your body creates more space for everything needed to keep your cognitive functions in top shape.
- **Increased Confidence Levels:** When the limitations of anxiety and stress no longer bind you, your confidence levels will soar, further contributing to the production of the beneficial hormones that keep your physical, mental, and spiritual health in check.
- **Enhanced Emotional Functions:** Expressing your emotions helps you process them, regardless of their origins or impact on your life. Journaling allows you to connect with your inner needs - enabling you to see which emotions you have used, and which should be discarded after the initial processing phase. Compartmentalizing negative feelings leaves enough room for developing positive ones that carry long-term benefits for your health and happiness.
- **Promotes Self-Discovery:** Through writing, you'll discover what makes you sad and what causes you joy, encouraging you to seek different experiences and learn more about yourself. You will notice the subtle changes caused by each positive event or emotion. This will also help you figure out your purpose and next step toward reaching it.
- **Improved Social Connections**: By developing a more realistic map of your feelings, you will learn how to manage the emotions you express towards others. It will also teach

you how to deal with the emotional responses you receive from your environment, encouraging you to develop stronger interpersonal relationships.

Inner Child Journaling

While keeping a journal can seem like a lot of work, it doesn't necessarily have to be. By following this simple guide, you can get to know your inner child and reveal the pain they are hiding in no time.

Here is what you should do:

1. Start by finding a space where you won't be disturbed for at least 20 minutes.
2. Prepare your journal and a pen and place them beside you as you sit comfortably.
3. Relax your shoulders, close your eyes, and visualize your inner child. Try to make the image as vivid as possible, as this will help you with the next step.
4. State your intention in your mind or out loud. Here you can ask your inner child about the emotions or thoughts you can't understand, or you can request guidance for spiritual development.
5. Release your intention by exhaling deeply and waiting for a response.
6. Keep an open mind about what you might receive - the answers may not arrive in the way you may expect them to.
7. Listen to your inner child's message, and don't forget to express your gratitude for their assistance.
8. Open your eyes and write down what you've learned immediately after receiving it. This will help you memorize the advice or instructions. By doing so, you will be able to honor it as closely as possible in the future.
9. After recording the message, take a deep breath and bring your focus back to the present.

Of course, following these steps will only be helpful if you have a clear intention and know which questions you should ask your inner child. Here are some great examples of how to comply with both of these requirements:

- Think about the activities you enjoyed as a child and whether you stopped doing them. If yes, ask your inner child why you shy away from that particular activity.
- Describe a situation in which you felt uncomfortable as a child and consider what you would tell your former self about this.
- Make sure to ask about the most trying thing you went through as a child and how you can release the pain caused by this event.
- Think about a place that made you feel safe as a child, and ask yourself whether you still feel the same way about them.
- Ask your inner child about favorite books, music, movies they like, and the heroes they admire.
- Inquire about your inner child's relationship with childhood friends and family members to see if any of them hurt you, causing you to internalize your feelings.
- Ask if someone else hurt you and whether you forgive them.
- Consider your current outlook on life and compare it to your childhood memories. Pay attention to differences in dreams and aspirations and what caused the changes.
- Ask your inner child if they are afraid of or anxious about something and what you can do to alleviate their fears.
- Ask the child how to treat them and provide them with the love they need to heal both of you.

Additional Tips for Inner Child Journaling

You can journal any time of the day you feel the need to, but for the best result, it's recommended to do this either after waking up or right before going to bed. Your mind will typically be confronted with numerous unanswered questions before going to sleep. Exploring and recording your insecurities, fears, or memories of old trauma before bedtime will help you put all those unanswered questions to rest. This will allow you to sleep better during the night and be healthier and more productive during the day. If any of the questions remain unanswered, your mind may resolve them on its own by processing the information you've got from your inner child.

You can also journal in the morning if you still have troubling thoughts or emotions when you wake up. If you are skeptical about the benefits of inner child journaling, performing the practice at least twice a day should help you notice its benefits soon enough. In fact, you don't even have to wait until bedtime or morning to journal. You can do it anytime you feel that you have to eliminate something from your system, even if you aren't sure what this is. You don't have to carry your journal with you all the time, either. Just keep a pen and a piece of paper with you so you can perform a quick inquiry and write down whatever you received as a response. You can copy this later in your journal so it can allow you to reread it carefully and contemplate its meaning.

You don't have to be a professional writer or possess creative writing skills to start journaling. Your entries don't have to be anything formal, just relevant to the questions you are asking your inner child. This means that you only need to write whatever association your brain makes first. Avoid contemplating the meaning of what you experience during the visualization process. Instead, document anything that comes to mind first, as honestly and succinctly as possible. If you find it easier to record the message or parts of it in pictures, feel free to draw it, starting from your inner child. Pay attention to the child's appearance, demeanor, and physical environment.

Creating a vivid image of your inner child helps focus your intention on them and will make it easier to draw your inner child in your journal next to some crucial entries. By immortalizing the child in your journal, you are creating tangible evidence of your eternal connection. Looking at their image will allow you to form a deeper bond, decipher their messages and prepare for other ones in the future. Draw the inner child in color to prevent your clear view of them from fading. Make sure to add any detail that stands out, such as an object they are holding or even a reference to the place or item they are showing you in their message. This is recommended for beginners who struggle with deciphering the meaning of spiritual messages if they have them written down in a journal. You don't necessarily have to draw a picture when communicating with your inner child. However, doing it as often as you can helps you understand their struggles so you can make them (and yourself) happier.

Journaling can be combined with other techniques, such as meditation, mindfulness, spiritual awareness, and affirmation techniques. Incorporating positive affirmations into your journaling practice will encourage you to give your inner child all the love they deserve. Right after you express your gratitude for the answer or guidance you received, you can say something like this:

> *"Now, I release the negativity from my body, mind, and soul.*
>
> *I'm happy to let go of all these things and move on.*
>
> *The wounds on my soul will only encourage me to become the best version of myself.*
>
> *I believe myself capable of everything I put my mind to - including letting go of unhealthy situations and undeserving people.*
>
> *I free myself from all these things because I deserve to be happy."*

Initially, one journal should suffice for all your thoughts. However, after practicing it for a while, you may want to think about two separate journals. In one, you can record all your negative emotions and troubling thoughts. The second one should be the place for expressing gratitude for all the positivity you experience. In the beginning, you should simply start your entries with the negative aspects and end them with the positive ones in the same journal. Try imagining your life as a journey with obstacles and rewards - all of which you encounter for a specific reason. Whether some hurt you or made you feel better, accept it and move on. Whatever material and spiritual gifts you receive, be grateful for them. Remember that not everyone is so lucky to have all those things. After all, healing your wounded inner child is accepting yourself for who you are, what you have, and what you can do with your newfound spiritual gifts.

After a while, your relationship with your inner child will improve - and you will learn to decipher their messages immediately. You won't need to read your entries about your experiences a couple of times to understand them, as you probably have to do when you start journaling. Not only that, but with enough practice, after writing down all the negative things, you will be able to move to the second part -

expressing your gratitude for everything you have experienced (good or bad) when visualizing your inner child.

Chapter 7: Inner Child Awareness

Do you think you are self-aware? Most people will answer "yes" because they aren't really familiar with the concept of self-awareness. However, experiencing true self-awareness is rare; only a few people know who they are and are rarely attuned to different parts of their personalities. Your wounded soul is a part of your true self, so when you become self-aware, you achieve inner child awareness as well.

Awareness is being present in the here and now without any concerns about the past or worries about the future. Most of us are never really "present" or living in the moment; our minds are always wandering somewhere else. This is the result of living a fast-paced life and always thinking of what we are going to do next. When was the last time you were truly focused on what you were doing? Do you remember the last time you drank coffee and were fully aware of the taste and the smell? When you go for a walk, are you aware of your legs moving and your heart beating? Or are you thinking only of the destination?

Your inner child lives in your unconscious mind, where all your past trauma and experiences are stored. We rarely pay attention to it, although it can help us learn so much about ourselves. Through awareness, you will be able to recognize negative emotions like anxiety or anger and access the subconscious mind to find their origins. This will help you manage these emotions instead of suppressing them or letting them take over. If you aren't aware and focused on your inner self and the world around you, you will not be able to pay attention to your inner child and heal its pain.

Inner child awareness is being able to focus inward on your emotions, thoughts, and actions and how they relate to your wounded soul. It usually raises the question, "Do my actions and thoughts align with what I am truly feeling?" This can lead you to determine if what you are feeling is the result of your inner child taking over or not. Some people are naturally self-aware and attuned to their inner self and inner child. They can easily evaluate their emotions and understand their triggers which can help them manage their reactions and be in control.

Being aware of your inner child will help you objectively perceive your emotions. Simply put, you will not be mad at your inner child or feel guilty or ashamed of it. You will be objective and understanding of your wounded soul's pain. Even after you discover your inner child, you may not be truly aware of it at all times. You may not always interpret it as your inner child behind certain actions, especially in the heat of the moment. However, when you practice inner child awareness, you can check on yourself to see where these feelings are coming from.

Inner child awareness will play a huge role in your healing as it will enable you to constantly check on your wounded soul during the day to see if it is happy, sad, or triggered by something. You will also be aware of your wounded child's strengths and weaknesses and how your actions impact the people in your life as well. This awareness will motivate you to take advantage of your strengths to grow and work on your weaknesses to heal.

Naturally, you will be curious about its reactions and triggers after connecting with your inner child. For instance, if you always tense up or feel anxious around a sibling or a family member, you may find these feelings confusing, and you will want to explore them to get to their roots. Inner child awareness will help you tap into your memories and realize that this family member may be used to bully or belittle you as a child, which is why you feel nervous every time you are around them. That said, being aware of your inner child can also help you experience more positive childhood feelings like joy or feeling carefree.

When we become aware of our inner child, we may experience feelings of guilt because we have neglected this wounded part of ourselves for so long. However, we will also sympathize with it and begin treating it with more love and compassion.

To always be aware and focused, you should practice awareness in every aspect of your life, like walking, sitting, eating, breathing, etc. Once you become aware of the world around you and the world within you, it will be easier for you to pay attention and stay focused on your inner child.

We have mentioned in previous chapters that our inner child wants attention and is always trying to communicate with us its needs. Are you listening to your inner child? Do you understand it is asking for help? Inner child awareness will open your senses so you can listen to your wounded soul when it is in pain and needs tending to. You can embrace it and let it know you will no longer neglect it. You can do this through writing, speaking to it, or even crying if this is going to be therapeutic.

The Positive Impact of Inner Child Awareness

According to research psychologist and author Diana Raab, inner child awareness will help you remember simpler times and the joy and innocence of childhood. When you tap into these emotions, you will be able to handle many of the challenges you face as an adult.

Discovering your inner child isn't easy for some people. Realizing a part of yourself is wounded can be hard, so instead of working on themselves to heal, they choose to suppress their feelings and ignore their inner child altogether. However, with awareness, you will be able to recognize this part of yourself rather than fight it. We can use awareness to embrace our inner child as well to give it the validation it has always wanted. Additionally, awareness requires you to be focused and present, enabling you to recognize the source of your pain and take the appropriate steps toward your healing.

Simply put, inner child awareness helps you recognize your inner child, embrace it, and heal it. Focusing on your daily activities will make looking inward and having better insight into your inner child easier.

Practicing awareness has always played a huge role in helping people heal from their trauma. You may be angry, sad, or hurt, but you aren't aware of it because you don't pay attention to your feelings or thoughts. As you become more conscious and aware of your inner self, you will be better equipped to work on your healing. In fact, various scientific studies have shown the benefits of awareness on our mental health and improving our wellbeing.

Our wounded inner child may be suffering from various mental health issues like depression, anxiety, stress, or trauma. Practicing awareness can improve your mental health so your inner child can heal from its past experiences and trauma.

Reduces Anxiety and Stress

Do you suffer from anxiety every time you have to speak in public, attend family gatherings, or stand up for yourself? This can be the result of a traumatic experience in your childhood. When you are aware of being anxious and stressed, you can consciously choose to work on your anxiety or lower your stress levels. You can achieve this by responding differently when you are stressed or working on remaining in control of your emotions rather than letting them control you and act out as a result.

Become Empathetic toward Your Inner Child

Inner child awareness allows you to be attuned to what your wounded soul is always feeling, especially when it is hurting and asking for help. This vulnerable part of yourself wants its feelings to be validated. By becoming aware of its pain, you will show empathy toward this broken part inside of you. Once you become empathetic, you will be more understanding of your inner child's needs to work on meeting these needs and thus healing.

Make Better Decisions

We have discussed in previous chapters how your inner child affects your decisions. As you become more aware of your wounded soul, you will better understand where your decisions are coming from. You will know if a decision stems from your inner child's fear or your adult self. Realizing your trauma is the driving source behind some of your reckless decisions will help you make better ones with a clear mind and without being influenced by your pain.

Self-Control

Your inner child is driven by pain and anger. Just like a child, it has no control over its emotions and throws tantrums every chance it gets. Inner child awareness will help you know when your thoughts, feelings, and reactions are irrational. Therefore, instead of reacting or losing your temper, you will take control of your emotions and respond rationally and calmly instead.

Change Bad Habits

As a result of your trauma, your wounded soul has acquired bad habits like self-criticism, belittling yourself, and the inability to say no. Being aware of your inner child will help you notice these habits, so you can change your thought patterns and, thus, your habits. For instance, if a friend asks you to pick them up from the airport but you have a job interview, your inner child will influence you to say yes because you are a people pleaser. However, by practicing inner child awareness, you will realize that you don't have to say yes to everything, especially when it inconveniences you. You will be aware that your inner child is afraid of standing up to itself and saying no. So, you will set healthy boundaries and learn when to say yes and when to say no without feeling guilty.

Change Your Perspective and Thought Patterns

Your inner child is still stuck in the past with the same childlike personality, looking at the world from the perspective of a scared and vulnerable kid. Because your thoughts haven't evolved or changed since you were a child, you may not be aware there is something wrong with the way you think or see the world. After you discover your inner child and embrace it, you can practice inner child awareness, tap into its thought pattern, and learn more about yourself and your inner child's pain. Whenever you have a negative thought, instead of giving in to it, take control and try to figure out what has brought these thoughts on. Are they the result of unrealistic worries? Do they stem from your pain and trauma? Once you take control and change your thought patterns, you can replace negative thoughts with more rational and positive ones.

Inner Child Awareness Guide

Practicing self-awareness isn't only effective, but it is also very easy and a great tool you can implement in your life to heal your inner child. In the next part of the chapter, we will provide simple exercises you can practice every day in various situations, so you are always aware of your inner child.

Ask Yourself Why

Before you make any decision, ask yourself, "Why am I making this decision?" and write down your answer. Give yourself a moment, ask yourself the same question a second and then a third time, and write down your answers. Take a look at the answers; are they rational? Are they good reasons? Do they stem from fear? Your answers will make it clear if you are making the right decision or influenced by your inner child's fear.

When your decisions are based on facts, you will feel confident with your choices and make better ones in life. The more you practice this technique, the more it will become second nature to you, and you will ask yourself the three whys each time. This will prevent your inner child from taking over whenever you're about to make a big decision.

Saying No to Your Inner Child

Your inner child should be treated with love and compassion, but just like a real child, you can't indulge in its every need. When you are aware of your inner child, you can tell the difference between your adult's self-demands and your wounded soul's demands. When you have unhealthy or irrational thoughts, this can be your inner child asking for something. You should only satisfy its health needs. For instance, if it wants you to turn to food to satisfy your emotional needs, throw a tantrum when your partner cancels a date, or spend money with no concern for the future, you should act like a strict parent and say "no."

Inner child awareness helps you see the difference between a child's needs and a mature person's needs. You will learn to reprogram your brain and re-parent your inner child by saying no to temptations and replacing bad or unhealthy thoughts and needs with healthy ones.

Think Before You Act

You have probably been told to think before you act. For many people, this is easier said than done. However, it can still be done with practice. Just like the three "whys" we have mentioned above to help you think before you make a decision, you should also pause and reflect before you act. Whenever we face a challenging or emotional situation, our inner child takes over and says things we shouldn't.

So, assess the situation and think objectively whenever you feel triggered or frustrated. This can be done by taking a few breaths before reacting to give yourself time to think clearly and assess the situation.

Watch Out for Negative Thoughts

Negative thoughts are the result of our fears and anxieties. They aren't rational, helpful, or have any base in reality. You should always be aware of these thoughts to determine their origin. For instance, if you aren't accepted in a job, you may think you are a failure instead of the more logical thinking that they probably went for someone with more experience. These thoughts stem from your vulnerable inner child, and all the time, a parent or teacher made you feel like you weren't good enough. Even when you achieve something, you will pass it off as luck instead of celebrating your successes.

Pay attention to your thoughts, and work on changing your thought patterns. Every time you achieve something, celebrate it even if you don't feel like it; this will reprogram your brain until celebrating your successes comes naturally to you. You should also forgive yourself and practice self-compassion each time you make a mistake instead of criticizing or being hard on yourself. Being aware of your wounded inner child and its thoughts is the only way to notice its negativity so you can replace them with a positive attitude.

Identify Your Triggers

There is always a reason for feeling anxious, angry, or frustrated during certain situations. In most cases, something has triggered your inner child, which manifested in these feelings. For instance, you feel anxious before every work meeting but don't pay attention to why you feel this way, so you never question it. By practicing inner child awareness, you can become aware of what triggered these feelings of anxiety. Maybe just the thought of having to speak up in a meeting was triggering. It reminded you of all the times you spoke up during family gatherings, and they would either make jokes or dismiss your opinions. By identifying your triggers, your adult self can take over by thinking logically and not letting your inner child use fear to hold you back.

Your triggers can also be a person or a place. Be conscious of your negative emotions and how you respond to your environment. Every time you experience a negative feeling, ask yourself: Why did I feel (angry, jealous, frustrated, sad, etc.) when talking to this person? Did they say something to make me feel this way? How did I react? Have I felt these emotions before? The answers will help you identify if your trigger was the person, tone of voice, or something they said. You can compare this situation to something you experienced in your childhood to understand why you feel this way now. If it is a person or a place that triggers you, you can avoid them, if possible.

Meditation

Meditation is known to help you clear your mind, stay focused, and be present in the here and now. You will find many mediation techniques that require you to be focused on your breathing. Even if you don't have time for meditating, you can simply take a couple of minutes at any time of the day to focus on your breathing. You can practice meditation by focusing on your breathing when you wake up before you go to sleep or in the car before you drive to work. When you focus on your breathing, you will begin to be more mindful and aware of your surroundings and everything you do. We have provided meditation techniques in this book, and you can also find various methods online or download meditation apps.

Evaluate Yourself

Check on yourself every once in a while to see if your inner child awareness is improving or not. You can also write down all the times that awareness has helped your inner child with its healing. Are you more aware, or are you still struggling? You can speak with a therapist if you have difficulty with inner child awareness.

Inner child awareness is an easy and effective method to heal your wounded soul. As you become focused on the present moment, your environment, and your inner child, you will be able to assess your wounded soul's emotions and reactions. Simply put, your inner child will always be on your mind, so you can easily tap into its feelings instead of letting it take over. You will be the one in control.

Chapter 8: The Challenges of Healing Your Inner Child

Did you ever take the time to listen to the random, little voices inside your head? You know, these voices that sound much like the younger version of you? This is what inner child healing is all about. As you know, it doesn't matter how old you get or where life takes you. Your inner child will always be there to accompany you on your life journey. Your inner child, however, will show up whenever you're the most hurt or disappointed. It will resurface when your friend doesn't take your call. Your teenage self may speak louder if you and your friend get into an argument. Taking note of when your inner child makes itself heard and acknowledging what it says are among the most important steps of inner child work.

Inner child work, or healing, is among the most popular methods of addressing the feelings of rejection and the things you believe you lacked throughout your childhood. It is a way to come to terms with the needs your inner child never fulfilled and overcome the attachment wounds you grew up with. Regardless of what your childhood was like, the chances are that there's a younger part of yourself that feels as if no one loved it enough or the right way.

Inner child healing is similar to any type of inner healing. For one, it requires you to give your subconscious the space to guide the process. You need to dig deep into your being and explore your emotions. Inner work urges you to nudge the parts of you that others have forced you to conceal. Growing up, you may have felt the need to suppress certain sides of yourself because of other people's snarky remarks. By permitting yourself to explore yourself from within, you start to tear down your daily coping mechanisms, such as avoidance, isolation, or numbing your emotions. Only then can you accept, acknowledge, and incorporate your subconscious workings into your consciousness.

Inner child healing is commonly used in several types of therapy, including trauma therapy, sensorimotor psychotherapy, narrative therapy, and art therapy. The best thing about this healing approach is that it encourages you to speak to your inner child in the language that it speaks. This means you will need to embody your emotions and let them guide you through these reflective conversations instead of expressing yourself through words and thoughts.

All of us traverse the world with the wounds we've developed throughout childhood. Even the simplest of traumas can affect us in significant ways. Everything, from neglect or emotional rejection to physical abuse, leaves its mark. We were always told to get over it or were made to believe that what we've experienced is "normal." This is why most of us never speak about our past experiences. We are left alone to experience the pain and emotions because "this is what adults are supposed to do."

Inner child work is vital because it always reminds us that our feelings are valid. We need the reassurance that our memory and feelings aren't wrong. It allows us to let the shame go and openly acknowledge these emotions. By healing your inner child, you are healing that little kid who felt neglected and the teen who cried every night because nobody understood them. When you're healing your inner child, you cultivate the safety, protection, and security that your younger child has always yearned for. In doing that, you alleviate some negativity your younger self has experienced, making room for positive experiences to emerge. Your natural, innate gifts, child-driven curiosity, and endless compassion are embraced.

However, avoiding acknowledging your past traumas leaves you feeling stuck and isolated. Repressing them only makes them worse because they will find other harmful ways to come out. Mental health issues and destructive mechanisms, such as alcoholism, substance abuse, workaholism, or even bullying and racism, occur. Inner child problems are often generational. This is why you're not only healing yourself by doing this type of work. You are helping generations learn to make peace with who they essentially are.

In this chapter, we will explore the challenges that come with the process of healing the inner child. You'll learn what to expect and read through some tips on how to work through them. Then, you'll find a multiple-step guide to navigating the challenges of inner child work.

The Challenges of Inner Child Work

Healing your inner child is not an easy endeavor. The process is very long and challenging. Though, many people don't realize that the main issue lies within the fact that the people who have hurt you will never help you heal. As an adult, you probably realize that you must go about this process independently. Healing starts from within, and you're the only one who can help yourself overcome these hardships. However, your subconscious or inner child doesn't grasp that. As a kid, you had complete blind trust in those around you, especially your family and the ones you loved the most. You looked up to them and sought them out for guidance. This is why the kid in you waits for the solution to come *from them.* After all, your parents probably jumped in to help you fix every problem you get yourself into.

You need to help the child in you realize that you need to work with them to heal their wounds. Your subconscious needs to make peace with the fact that there will be no one to come in to apologize and help you pick up the pieces they broke. Most adults will never admit that they hurt you in your childhood. Your parents will likely never acknowledge that they may have wronged you or were unsuccessful in their attempt at parenthood. Fortunately, there are many ways to go on about the heavy responsibility of healing the child within you. But first, let's look at some challenges you may face throughout this journey.

1. The Lack of Common Trust

Your inner child has been let down one too many times. They had unquestionable trust in the same people who initially betrayed them. This is why your inner child will not warm up to you easily. Yes, even when you are the older version. We are usually our strongest and most potent enemy. We constantly criticize, shame, and hurt ourselves. You have probably invalidated your emotions or shamed yourself for feeling the way you do at one point in your life. The only way you can get your child to come out of its hiding place is by proving to them that you're their ally and friend. You need to be supportive and non-critical. Most importantly, you need to acknowledge and validate their feelings and everything that they went through, no matter how much society normalizes it. Recognizing your younger self's neglect, abuse, abandonment, and loneliness is essential to healing.

In other words, be the adult that your younger self needs. You were supposed to be cared for while growing up. Instead, you ended up wounded. It's easy to feel like the damage can't be undone, especially when you have no idea where to start. The journey is long, and you need to tackle many aspects of your current and past self. On the other hand, you are an adult now. You need to trust your ability to care for yourself and offer your inner child the type of care that they deserve. Think about what went wrong and the things that hurt you as a child, and what could've made things better for you. For instance, if your parents used to abuse you verbally, your inner child would need someone to respect, encourage, and support them. This is how you need to approach your younger self. Retreat to a quiet place and have a conversation with your inner child out loud. Tell them everything they want to hear. Express your love for your inner child and tell them that you're proud of them.

2. The Need for Validation

It is sometimes hard to separate your own thoughts and feelings from those around you. We are automatically influenced by the mindsets and beliefs of our community. We adopt many ideas as our own even when we don't entirely agree with them. This is why you may still be inclined toward trivializing or even justifying how you were hurt. You will manage to find a reason for the way you were shamed, abandoned, or forced to grow up before your time. You may even tell yourself that your experiences weren't that bad. This is why you need to take a step back and ask yourself whether these claims are coming from your authentic self or are influenced by the world around you. Because if they were your own, you wouldn't be reading this book and trying to figure out how to heal your inner child. If these hurtful actions were justifiable, or what you experienced wasn't "that bad," then you wouldn't feel hurt in the first place. Acknowledge that whatever you've gone through wounded you. If it makes you feel any better, your parents did not nurture you how they had to, not because they're bad people, but because they, too, have wounded inner children.

Make your inner child feel seen and listen to their hardships. Knowing that you're loved and feeling the love are never the same. Your younger self needs to feel the love. It needs to know that people see who they really are and understand that they are cared for. It's up to you to do so. Fortunately, there is plenty you can do to make up for that now that you're no longer a child. Think about how your inner child reacts in the face of challenges, fears, the things that make them happy, etc. Be attentive to them.

3. Dealing with the Stages of Grief

Shock and anger are the beginning stages of grief, which, believe it or not, is a sign that you're heading in the right direction. Anger and shock are very normal feelings, even if you understand that whatever you've experienced in your childhood was never intentional. Anger is a standard element in the inner wounded child healing process. You don't need to break things or scream at the top of your lungs (however, if you need to, that's fine too), but it's your right to be very mad.

If you think about it, your parents probably did the best job any two adults with a wounded inner child can do. However, this doesn't mean that you're any less emotionally and spiritually hurt by how things went down. This is exactly why you need to realize that it's up to you to hold a generation of wounded children accountable to stop hurting themselves and those around them.

Stand up for the younger version of you whenever someone offends or belittles them in any way. Now, it wouldn't be possible to travel back in time (although that would accelerate the healing process or even deflect the damage), but you can stand up for yourself right now, especially when someone belittles you in a way that your inner child was used to. For instance, if you were frequently told how dramatic you were, then be sure to stand up for yourself if someone says that to you now. Let them know their limits and explain that this is something you don't appreciate hearing. Make your inner child proud to know that you no longer tolerate any type of disrespect.

4. The Waves of Sadness

You will inevitably experience deep waves of anger and sadness after you're done feeling angry. You'll likely grieve the life you could've lived if you weren't still dealing with the consequences of your past wounds. You'll feel a sense of regret regarding all your childhood dreams, ambitions, and aspirations. It's okay to grieve the unfulfillment of everything that you haven't developed healthily.

It helps involve your inner child in your journey. After all, you need their cooperation to make it past the healing phase. By now, you should be able to tell what makes your inner child happy. You don't need to have everything covered, nor do you need to know everything about your inner child. This entire journey is a learning experience. This means you'll find something new about your younger self every day. Use your scope of knowledge to do the things your inner child likes as frequently as you can. It's easy to ignore your inner child when trying to become the adult you "ought to be." What we don't realize, however, is that this worsens the situation. The more we repress the desires of our inner child, the more prominent they become. Eventually, you won't be able to push them aside, as they will leave you feeling irritated, relentless, and hopeless. If you've been doing that for a long time, you may even end up experiencing an identity crisis. This is a sign that you need to align your behavior with your needs.

5. Remorse Kicks In

Remorse is a very strong emotion that kicks in whenever we've lost something. It is often experienced after the loss of a loved one. However, it is also relevant in your case because your inner child may start to wonder if they could've done anything differently. You need to help your subconscious realize the fact that there was nothing that your younger self could've done to change how things went down. Let your inner child know that their pain should be about them and not what could've been. They were never responsible for what they went through. They couldn't have been a better child to their parents. It was their job to give your inner child a healthy upbringing, and it's your job, as an adult, to let your inner child know just that.

6. You'll Feel Lonely

Perhaps the strongest feelings you'll experience throughout this journey are profound shame and loneliness. Your parents abandoning or abusing you is shameful to you. You feel bad about yourself and likely believe that there's something wrong with you because this is how they treated you. This shame eventually leads to loneliness. Your inner child feels like they're an alien. They feel contaminated, and so they will hide their authentic self from the world, putting on a mask in the process. Your inner child lives the rest of his life as an imposter, which makes them feel lonely and misunderstood.

This is the last and longest step in the healing process. It is the most challenging to endure. However, there is a way out, which is to seek therapy. You need to reach out to a professional to deal with your shame and loneliness healthily. These feelings are hard to acknowledge on our own. Though, acknowledgment and acceptance are necessary if you want to overcome these obstacles. It is the only way you'll finally reconnect with your long-lost true self.

Navigate the Challenges of Inner Child Healing

The following is a multiple-step guide you can use to navigate the challenges that come with inner child work:

1. Acknowledge Your Inner Child

If you want to start healing, you must acknowledge that your inner child is there and hurting. Be open to the idea of exploring the past, so you don't further complicate the healing process. You may struggle with approaching your younger self at first. This is why it helps to explore your most significant childhood experiences first. Accept that they happened, dig deep into how they made you feel, and then talk to your inner child as if they were a real, separate person.

2. Be an Active Listener

Listen to the feelings that arise during your conversation. Be attentive to emotions like anger, loneliness, insecurity, shame, anxiety, and guilt, and interpret what they are trying to say to you. Try to trace them back to some events or even people in your life. Think about the situations that trigger similar emotions in your adult self. Do you sense a pattern?

3. Try Journaling or Writing a Letter

Now that you're grown, you probably have a different perspective than you did back then, especially when it comes to the events or situations that wounded you. Writing them down can help you address the things your inner child doesn't fully grasp. Let's say you may have always feared your brother because he was an angry child. If you now know that he was subject to years of bullying, you may help your inner child understand that your brother's anger was never against the child in you. Ask your inner child about their feelings and how they would like you to support them.

4. Meditate

Now that you've asked your inner child some questions, it is time to meditate. This will help you bring answers to light. Meditation is known to heighten a person's self-awareness by teaching you to direct your focus to the emotions that arise during the day. Meditation is all about mindfulness, which makes it easier to spot the events that trigger unwanted actions.

Loving your inner child doesn't happen overnight, nor does healing your wounds. You may not realize it now; however, once you embark on the healing journey, you will realize that inner child work is all about loving the younger version of yourself. It doesn't matter how odd, shy, difficult, annoying, loud, or weird you thought (or were told) you were. You did, and you still deserve love. You don't need a time machine to return and let your inner child know they are worth the world.

Chapter 9: The Benefits of Healing Your Inner Child

Connecting with your inner child can do wonders. It may sound like an exaggeration; however, you can transform your life by healing that little kid inside you. You will never fully realize how much your wounded inner child was holding you back until you completely heal. You will look back and wonder how you were traversing life with that much weight strapped to your shoulders.

Inner child work allows you to forgive and move forward. You learn to acknowledge what your parents did to you without blaming them for the way you turned out. Healing your inner child comes with a different level of maturity where you don't deny the impact of your upbringing but still understand that this is the best your parents could've done. The healing process will help you come to terms with the fact that there's nothing you could've done to stop this from happening. When all the work is done, you will see that you are responsible for taking the initiative and changing certain aspects of your life. You simply don't have to settle for the way things are. You will no longer be a victim of your own sadness or experiences, nor will you allow yourself to be overtaken by feelings of resentment, which leads us to the next point.

Inner child work is empowering. It will urge you not to allow self-doubt and fear to guide you. Instead, you will learn to take the reins when it comes to your emotions and reactions. A great part of healing your inner child depends on how you defend your current and younger selves whenever you need to. You would no longer use your past traumas as excuses to indulge in destructive behaviors. This type of healing will help you let go of your old, unwanted habits. When you're empowered, you will no longer want to live as a victim who blames their destructive coping mechanisms on their past traumas.

The healing process comes with its fair share of pain and discomfort. However, if there's one thing you'll learn, it's that the greatest amount of healing comes when you're outside of your comfort zone. In this chapter, you'll learn about the benefits of healing your inner child and how you can achieve them. Here, you will also find a quiz that will help you pinpoint which benefits you have experienced by practicing healing your wounded soul.

Benefits of Inner Child Work

No matter what you do, nothing will stop you from acting like a child unless you do some serious inner child work. No amount of anger or time management, breathing, or meditative techniques will help you improve your attention, acknowledge and control your emotions, and hold yourself accountable instead of blaming and accusing others, communicating effectively, and jumping to conclusions. Although these techniques can offer great complimentary support, you must first address your main problem: healing your wounded inner child. Once you start healing your inner child, you'll witness your life-changing right before your eyes. You may feel pressured to do everything by the book. However, in this journey, no one is perfect. There isn't a standard healing practice that you can benchmark your efforts against in the first place. As long as you're connecting with your inner child, validating their emotions, and being the parent they deserve and long for, you will be able to reap the benefits of self-love, compassion, self-awareness, and emotional control. The following are some of the benefits of doing inner child work:

1. Acknowledging the Pain

You will never truly understand the pain and the extent of its impact unless you hear from the wounded. You need to create a safe space for them to talk about how they feel as they reflect on their emotions. You can do that by prioritizing safety in the relationship you build with your inner child. Make them feel safe, loved, and important. Approach them with respect and validation so they can warm up to you. Only then can you penetrate the layers of accumulated wounds, reflecting on each revelation you make. Take it slow and work at your inner child's pace. Never push boundaries or go beyond your and your inner child's pain thresholds. Otherwise, you will compromise that trust.

2. Exploring Your Boundaries

There are many aspects to healing your inner child. It's a very dynamic journey. Your feelings, needs, and desires may change multiple times throughout the process, depending on the traumas, memories, and experiences you encounter. You must remember that you're working with your inner child throughout the years. For instance, your emotional and developmental needs at the age of 6 are quite different from your needs at the age of 14. Whenever you're working with your inner child, make sure to take note of their emotional age. Then, generate your boundaries, tailoring them to each version of yourself. Regardless of what your needs are, approach them without judgment.

Exploring your boundaries throughout the years gives you a lot of insight into the person you are today. It helps you better understand your needs, preferences, and dislikes. It will also help you determine what your current boundaries are in life.

3. Working Your Way toward Wholeness

If you're struggling with a wounded inner child, you haven't experienced wholeness yet. Unresolved pains and traumas make it impossible for you to find and embrace all parts of yourself. You lead your life in fragments of your being. Have you ever noticed how it's easy for you to set aside a part of yourself whenever you have to? Healing your inner child is a lot like searching for a lost kid. You look everywhere, trying to trace the steps back and putting clues together until you finally find them. You achieve wholeness when you've successfully brought back the child and found that it coexists harmoniously with your adult self. While it's easier said than done, the only piece of advice we can give you here is to sit tight. Patience is a virtue. You embarked on this journey knowing that it won't be easy. Whenever you feel like you want to give up, remember why you started in the first place. Think of the child who deserved better growing up. Remind yourself that you can't let them down again.

4. Identifying Narcissism

Many of those who experience childhood trauma end up falling victim to narcissistic abuse and toxic relationships. This is often a survivor's coping method or trauma response. This is especially the case if you grew up with narcissistic caregivers who desensitized you to this type of unacceptable behavior. Being constantly exposed to it as a child probably led you to believe that it was normal. A significant aspect of inner child work is understanding your trauma response patterns. You will learn a lot about safe and toxic relationships when you discover how they developed in the first place and how they helped you in life. This will make it easier for you to spot narcissists and avoid falling into the same traps.

5. No More Tantrums

If you are yet to heal your inner child, then the occasional emotional meltdown is probably no stranger to you. Keeping track of your triggers and tracing them back to certain memories, correlations, stories, or events can help you break the emotional outburst cycle before it occurs. Suppose someone, for instance, says something that you now realize would trigger an undesirable reaction. In that case, you should be ready to distract your inner child or deflect their reaction. Going for a long walk, retreating to a safe space, meditating, or doing breathing exercises are all preventative measures. It will take some experimentation until you find something that works for the child inside.

"Paradoxical anger" is another type of anger. Every time you were angry with your parents, you probably repressed your emotions. Your feelings weren't something that you could easily express because lashing out would've come with consequences. Unfortunately, the same people who compromised your boundaries, sense of security, and trust are the ones that your younger self depended on. As you do inner child work, you need to find positive ways in which you can release the repressed anger while preventing emotional outbursts.

As you may recall from the previous chapter, you need to take the time to explore your inner child's wants and desires. Figure out what makes them happy, calm, and relaxed. This would give your insight into the activities you need to do to prevent outbursts.

6. Attaining Freedom from Toxic Shame

Think about your current life and reflect on your life as a teenager. What are the thoughts that preoccupy your brain? When you think about yourself as a child, what comes to mind? Is it a shame? Feelings of inadequacy?

How often do you catch yourself shaming your younger self? You may find yourself reflecting on how imperfect you were and how you could've done better to make your parents proud. Maybe you think of all the rash decisions you took when you were 16 and all the things you did that didn't match your values. The only way to free yourself from toxic shame is to externalize these emotions. Talking about your past can help you get rid of the shame and replace it with compassion.

7. Being Your Own Parent

When you're doing inner child work, you must treat your inner child as a child of your own. You need to nurture it and care for it. This means you can be the parent you lacked as a child. You get to do things right this time around, ensuring that you meet your younger self's developmental needs. Be the person your inner child can depend on, connect with, and confide in. You are their only shot at getting heard, finding safety, and feeling loved unconditionally.

8. Breaking Unhealthy Cycles

Have you ever wondered why it's often those who had unstable childhoods are the ones that end up in codependent and unhealthy relationships? Well, it's because people with somewhat similar struggles are subconsciously attracted to each other. They are drawn to what's familiar, and together, they relive moments from their childhoods.

As children, we were helpless and completely dependent on our parents. We looked up to them and believed that they were always right. This is why we automatically thought it was our fault when troubles arose. We came up with beliefs and assumptions about ourselves that we carried into adulthood. We also created strategies that we thought would help us get whatever we needed from our parents. We still resort to these strategies in all our relationships. We inadvertently recreate the chaos we grew up with to ensure that our behaviors, thoughts, and actions are still relevant. Knowing what to expect and maintaining a sense of familiarity provide us with a false sense of safety and security.

You need to discover which patterns you fall into to make a conscious choice. While it will be extremely uncomfortable at first, you must go out of your comfort zone to show your inner child that you don't need to recreate the same environment they were brought up in or refer to the same strategies to be safe.

9. Determining Your Self-Worth

Unfortunately, we live in a world where our value is determined by what we do rather than who we are. The world is utterly role-based. It's sad to see that families - where members are supposed to have unconditional love and respect for each other - follow the same construct. From a young age, we are taught to let go of our individuality and set aside our hobbies, talents, and complete identities so we can adopt traits that would make our parents proud. We are encouraged to appeal to the world instead of being ourselves.

Our parents taught us that the things we like and love (the things that essentially make us who we are) come second to our "role." You probably spent your whole childhood trying to perfect the role that they had mapped out for you. You did your best to overachieve, whether it came to your academics, athletics, or chores, thinking that this was what you wanted. Unfortunately, being an overachiever is seldom a personal choice. It rather sprouts from the need to please one's parents. If you have an older sibling, then they're probably the ones who ended up on the overachiever train. Though, this probably didn't salvage you from unnecessary emotional damage. Instead of feeling pressured to excel at every aspect of life, you had to hear about what a "star" your sibling is, which likely made you feel inferior or useless.

Inner child work is your shot at making your inner child feel worthy and valued. You need to address your inner child using positive statements, highlighting how valuable their authentic self is. Explore your inner child's dreams and aspirations, comparing them to your parents' standards. Do you really want to be the person you strived to be? Reassure your inner child that they were born with a much greater purpose that only their unique and special gifts can help them fulfill.

10. Discovering Who You Truly Are

As we just explained, taking on that designated role cuts off your connection with the person you truly are. The moment you made it your mission to do everything you could to please your parents, you wiped out fragments of your being. The playful, curious, creative, imaginative, and spontaneous parts of yourself were diminished. You no longer carried around the healthy sense of shamelessness, innocence, and objectivity that every child should have. At a very young age, you were introduced to the concepts of self-criticism, guilt, and shame.

You need to take the time to reconnect with the younger version of yourself. Take as long as it takes to remember who you once were. Remember the kid who was not afraid to express themselves, go on adventures, take risks, and most importantly, play to your heart's content. Search for the part of you that enjoys life as it comes with all its ups and downs. Teach your inner child that obstacles or pitfalls don't compromise your safety but that they teach you to pick yourself up.

11. Get Rid of Your Sexual Guilt and Shame

In most cases, one's inner child suffers from severe sexual guilt and shame. These negative emotions are usually a product of family repression, bullying or ridicule, enmeshment, incest, and other traumas. Few people realize that our upbringing can greatly influence our sexuality as adults. These wounds can appear as sexual anorexia or the rejection of all types of intimate relationships, sexual addictions, an addiction to pornography viewing, etc.

When a child has been subject to incest or enmeshment, they will end up repressing their sexuality in hopes of pushing away the parent who had hurt them. Not only that, but further into adulthood, the individual will struggle with feelings of guilt when it comes to sexual relationships. This may stand in the way of building healthy romantic relationships. To help your inner child overcome this shame, you need to reassure them that it's not wrong to be curious about sex. They need to understand that sexual urges and drives are normal and that they're nothing to be ashamed of. Finally, they are now safe, meaning that they don't need to hide their sexuality from the offending caregiver anymore.

Quiz: Which Inner Child Healing Benefits Have I Experienced?

Use this quiz as a guide to help you measure your progress throughout the inner child healing journey.

- My overall quality of life has improved.
- I no longer suffer from mental cloudiness.
- My anxiety is not as severe as it used to be.
- I am experiencing fewer or diminished symptoms of depression.
- My vitality has improved.
- My sense of curiosity and wonder is now revived.
- I believe I can stand up for myself better.
- I have a clearer understanding of my boundaries, and I make sure that no one oversteps them.
- I can say "no" whenever I need to.
- I can cultivate better intrapersonal relationships.
- I am more emotionally mature and can control my feelings better.
- I am more "myself" than I was before.
- I am no longer ashamed of my past painful experiences.
- I don't feel guilty about my unhealthy coping mechanisms. I realize that, at one point, it was the only way I could've survived.
- I am not worried about what people think of me. I don't allow anyone's opinions to dictate my mental state.
- I don't feel resentful toward my family and the people who hurt me.
- I don't feel shameful when it comes to my sexuality.
- I can identify narcissistic behaviors and unhealthy patterns.
- I speak my mind and no longer repress my thoughts and feelings for fear of hurting someone.

You may not have really understood how relevant your inner child was until you decided to give this book a read. You were never aware of how big of a role your younger self plays in how you think, act, react, and feel today. However, once you start taking steps toward inner child work, you'd feel like you opened yourself up to a new world that you never knew existed. Inner child work is all about realizing that many of the emotions that we experience as adults, such as fear and insecurity, are brought over by the inner child. Today, you are grown and different from how you used to be. Because your younger self was never granted the right to have opinions, you grew up keeping them to yourself, denying yourself the ability to be assertive. Once you see that this fear comes from the child within, you can calm and soothe them. Being compassionate and understanding can, over time, help you overcome the fears that weigh you down. You will gain clarity and self-awareness in your efforts to heal your inner child.

Chapter 10: Healing Your Inner Child Challenge

Our emotions and overall happiness highly depend on our childhood experiences. Many people don't understand that they have to account for their childhood when planning for the future. We are spiritually connected with several versions of ourselves, which we must remember when deciding which way to go. This doesn't mean that you should stay stuck in the past or let previous negative events hold you back. We mean that you need to determine how your past influences your current life. Pinpointing unhelpful patterns, problematic behaviors, and detrimental coping mechanisms is the only way you'll get one step closer to leading a happier life. You need to explore how you were raised, find out how you make your choices, and evaluate the quality of your connections throughout the course of your life. If you don't take the time to figure out the state of your mental, emotional, social, and spiritual health, you'll never be able to tell what you need to do to change your life for the better and get rid of the things that hold you back from achieving the things you deserve.

Your inner child is a more critical part of your mind, joy, freedom, playfulness, friendliness, and compassion than you realize. This part of yourself represents the aspect of you that desires to feel loved, safe, comfortable, and protected. The reason why it's so relevant to your spiritual health is that it is a combination of your fundamental and innate emotions, imagination, creativity, and vulnerability that you repressed as you grew older. The inner child is, you guessed it, the childlike aspect of your being. It is the part of you that reacts impulsively or lashes out whenever things don't go how they want. It is basically everything you've learned and experienced during your developmental stages of life. The younger child inside is your essence. It is the intrinsically innocent, playful, and uncomplicated part of your consciousness.

Now that you understand that the concept of healing the inner child is an important step towards spiritual well-being and awakening, you are now prepared to go on about this process in the form of a challenge. This chapter serves as a 30-day guide to healing your inner child, ultimately allowing you to reach spiritual awakening.

Day 1: Identify Your Inner Child Archetype

- Do the "What Inner Child Archetype Am I?" Quiz. Complete the quiz in chapter 2 to determine your inner child's archetype.
- Detach. When identifying your inner child archetype, you need to be very mindful when it comes to what you're feeling and thinking. You need to be sure that you're exploring the beliefs and values that belong to you, not those imposed on you by your community or society. Detach yourself from the world around you and have a deep conversation with your inner child. Find out how they feel, what they're thinking about, what they need, which activities make them happy, etc.
- Practice Self-Compassion. Many people have the wrong idea about practicing self-compassion. The process isn't all about hyping yourself up or telling yourself that there's nothing to feel bad about. On the contrary, feeling bad is fine, just like feeling happy is okay. Self-compassion is all about developing mindfulness toward your childhood experiences and acknowledging the child within. This means that the last thing you should do is to play down your insecurities, sadness, or fears. Make sure you are present and let your inner child know they are wanted, loved, and valid.

Day 2: Practice Awareness of Your Inner Child

- Go for a long walk in nature. Taking a long walk in nature can help you feel grounded and in tune with your surroundings. It can also give you mental clarity and help you acknowledge your thoughts and emotions. Be fully present in the moment and engage all your senses.
- Practice Yoga. The Mountain is a very easy yoga pose that anyone can do. If you're more experienced with yoga, you can do any other pose you like as long as it makes you feel comfortable and focused. The Mountain pose can help you with your posture, body awareness, and alignment.
- Plant both feet flat on the floor as you stand up straight. Your heels should be parted as your big toes touch. Roll your shoulder blades down while lifting your chest. Move your chin inward as you elongate your head. Place your arms by your sides with your palms facing forward. Your throat should be constricted while you breathe through your nose. Maintain the pose for 5 to 10 breaths.
- Meditate. Meditate for 5 minutes before you go to bed.

Day 3: Journal about Your Inner Child

- Write a letter to your inner child. Write a letter to your younger self from the point of view of a loving, supportive parent. Explain how you will protect them and express how much you're proud of them. Tell them that you love them and are working on giving them the life and happiness they deserve. You can even apologize if you want to. Write from your heart.
- Write about your needs. Explore your younger self's sense of identity. Explore your most basic needs. What does your inner child long for? Is it love? Is it safe? Write about what your inner child needs to feel like themself.
- Come up with affirmations. Write affirmations expressing your value, unique traits, what you bring to the table, how

you affect other people's lives, etc.

Day 4: Embrace the Hurt

- Meditate. Meditate for 5 minutes in the morning.
- Reflect. Retreat to a quiet and safe space. Detach from your environment and shift your full attention to your emotions. How do you feel right now? Think about your childhood and how your memories make you feel. Has anything changed since you decided to embark on your inner child healing journey? Does it make you feel better or worse so far? Don't set your emotions aside, no matter how painful they may be. Acknowledge them and experience them fully.

Day 5: Engage Your Inner Child

- Spend time with children. Spend some time with kids and take part in activities they enjoy doing. If you have kids, give them a portion of your day. If you don't, you can offer to babysit your niece or a friend's child for the day. Don't be afraid to let your inner child come out.
- Let loose. Allow yourself to let loose today. If you're usually serious at work, it won't hurt to crack a joke or take things slow every once in a while. Be playful and have fun.
- Visualize. Visualize the future you want before you go to bed. Think about your future home, car, and job. How do you look? What does your style look like? Let your imagination run wild.

Day 5: Nurture Your Inner Child

- Have a conversation with your inner child. Acknowledge your inner child's presence and let them know that you wish to connect with them on a deeper level. Explain that their safety and comfort are your topmost priorities.
- Look at old photos. Look at old photos of yourself and say affirmations of protection, compassion, and love.
- Write about your decision to let go of old cycles. Write a letter to your inner child that includes everything they need

to hear. This can be an apology letter that addresses the fact that they had to grow up so fast or that they were never nurtured the way they should've been.

- Give them a safe space to play. Think about the type of games you always wished you could play as a child, and make sure to do just that.

Day 6: Validate Their Emotions

- Release your emotions. Grab your journal and write down all your feelings and emotions. Be as expressive and detailed as possible, allowing nothing to remain unacknowledged or slip through the cracks.
- Meditate. Meditate for 5 minutes.
- Take a break. Take the day off from work and responsibilities. Take it easy and go with the flow.
- Burn incense. Burning incense can serve as a great mood booster. It can also relieve stress and anxiety.
- Do something fun. Do anything you typically enjoy doing, whether it's practicing a hobby, going out with friends, or watching a movie.

Day 7: Re-Examine Our Boundaries

- Say no. Think before doing any favors or following others. Think about whether this is something you really want to do. Don't be afraid to turn down requests or invitations you're not up for.
- Reflect on your relationships. Think about all the relationships in your life. What are your familial, social, professional, and romantic relationships like? What does your definition of a healthy relationship look like? Do any of your relationships in life match that description? Do you feel uncomfortable when hanging around some people? Why is that? Would you describe any of your relationships as unhealthy? Why? What do you plan on doing about it?

- What are your boundaries? What are your boundaries when it comes to the way you interact with others? Are they different from your boundaries back then? Do you allow people to overstep your boundaries? If so, why do you do it, and how does it make you feel?

Day 8: Ground Yourself

- Take a long walk in nature and make sure you're present and connected with your surroundings.
- Practice yoga. You can do some light poses like The Mountain pose or Warrior I. If you're up for a challenge, watch a beginner's yoga video on YouTube and follow along.
- Burn sage.
- Practice deep breathing. Breathe deeply for 2 to 3 minutes.

Day 9: Get Moving

- Stretch. Do light stretches for 5 to 10 minutes.
- Exercise. Do your favorite form of exercise for 30 minutes.
- Go for the stairs. Take the elevator instead of the stairs. If you have a quick errand to run, walk or bike those few blocks instead of driving or taking a cab. Release your energy.

Day 10: Heal by Helping Others

- Lend someone a hand. Does a friend look like they have been struggling lately? Ask what you can do for them and try to help them out. Working on qualities like kindness and compassion is crucial when doing inner child work.
- Pet an animal or play with a baby.
- Smile at strangers.
- Do a random act of kindness.

Day 11: Take Control

- Come up with a to-do list. Write a to-do list of everything you need to do throughout the day. Prioritize the tasks from most to least important. If you have nothing to do today, it's time to work on any tasks you've been putting off.
- Declutter your home. Come up with a fun way to declutter your home. Not only will this instill a sense of accomplishment, but it will remind your inner child that responsibilities don't have to be burdensome.
- Detach. Let go of unhelpful thoughts and emotions.

Day 12: Manage Your Emotions

- Notice your feelings. Check in on your emotions multiple times throughout the day. Carry a mood journal around where you can write all about your emotions and the reactions they trigger.
- Meditate. Retreat to a safe space and meditate for 3 to 5 minutes whenever you need to.
- Practice deep breathing. Breathe deeply for 3 minutes several times during the day.
- Think before you react. Take a moment to think about whether it's the appropriate time and place to express your emotions.

Day 13: Practice Mindfulness

- Tune into your senses. Stop every once in a while to engage all your senses in your experiences. For instance, when you're eating, feel the texture of the food or how the spoon feels against your fingertips, savor the food with your eyes, enjoy its taste, take in its smell, and listen to the surrounding environment.
- Practice self-compassion. Treat yourself the way you would treat a friend.

- Shift your attention. Sit down for a minute whenever you're having negative thoughts and shift your attention to your breathing.

Day 14: Grow Your Self-Awareness

- Be objective. Think about yourself objectively. What are your accomplishments? Did the things that made you happy as a child still make you happy now?
- Think about your goals. What are your goals and plans for the future?
- Meditate. Meditate for 10 minutes before bed.

Day 15: Acknowledge Your Progress

- Practice deep breathing. Breathe deeply for 2 to 3 minutes.
- Stretch. Stretch lightly for 5 minutes.
- Journal. Write about your progress and what you've accomplished throughout this journey so far. How have the past 15 days changed you? What do you expect to achieve by the end of the challenge?
- Exercise. Do your favorite form of exercise for 15 minutes.
- Reward yourself. Reward your inner child for making it this far and do something that makes them happy.

Day 16: Release the Past

- Do an emotional release. Write down everything you're feeling and thinking about.
- Identify your emotional loop. Are there certain emotions that you experience every day? What triggers them? What can you do to counter them?
- Replace negative emotions with positive ones. Did you know that you can train yourself to feel positive emotions in situations that typically make you feel resentful or sad? If something doesn't turn out the way you hoped it would, you will undoubtedly feel bad. However, you can alleviate those

negative emotions and even eventually turn them into positive ones by reshaping your thought process. Instead of viewing this as a failure, you can think of it as a learning experience.

Day 17: Grow Your Trust

- Stop comparing. Stop comparing yourself to others.
- Don't worry about the opinions of others.
- Restructure your "What Ifs." Turn negative what-ifs like "what if I fail" into positive ones like "what if it works out for the best?"

Day 18: Connect with Your Inner Child

Dedicate this day to connecting with your inner child. Listen to everything they have to say and feel. Take the day off from work if you need to. Engage in activities that made you the happiest in your childhood. Explore your childhood wounds, where they came from, what feelings they're associated with, and what events trigger these feelings. Reassure your inner child that they're now safe and protected.

Day 19: Go Offline

- Exercise. Practice your favorite form of exercise for 15 minutes.
- Go offline. Take a break from electronics for the day.
- Go out for ice cream. Treat yourself to ice cream or stop by your favorite drive-through from your childhood on your way home.
- Get creative. Draw, paint, dance, or practice any other creative activity of your choice.
- Practice one of your hobbies.

Day 20: Forgive

Day 20 is all about forgiveness. Forgive someone who hurt you in your childhood. Think about what they did and how it made you feel.

Imagine these thoughts and emotions floating away and out of your mind. Forgive them for your own peace of mind. If you're not on talking terms with that person, you don't need to reach out to them if you don't wish to. Remember, you're forgiving them for your own good.

Day 21: Put Yourself First

- Meditate. Meditate for 5 minutes.
- Do something that makes your inner child happy.
- Say no. Say no to the things you don't want to do.
- Practice self-care. Take a long bath, a nap, visit a spa, or practice any other form of self-care.

Day 22: Fill the Gaps

What are some consequences you fell victim to in your childhood? Realize that these are things you can rise up against now that you're an adult. For instance, if you didn't receive adequate care as a child, you can take steps to ensure that you're always prioritized and cared for. If you grew up in poverty, you could come up with a financial plan, learn how to budget and save, and take steps to increase your income.

Day 23: Go on an Adventure

Whether you decide to go to the fair or pack your bags and leave the city for the day, you should do something spontaneous. Embrace your innate desire for adventure and allow your inner child inside to flourish. Bonus points if you manage to do something you've always wanted to do as a child!

Day 24: Stand Up for Yourself

- Practice self-love. Think about 4 qualities you like about your past and current self.
- Stand your ground. Don't be afraid to express your opinions even when others don't agree with them.
- Stand up for yourself. Defend yourself whenever someone disrespects you or looks down on you. Don't allow anyone to

insult you.

Day 25: Write a Letter

Write a letter to the people who left the most significant impact on you throughout your life. Focus primarily on your childhood. Write down how they made you feel and how they changed you for better or worse. Are there certain events that you associate with those people? What memories and emotions do those events trigger? What would you say to those people if you could speak up with no consequences? Once you're done, read it out loud and imagine that you're talking to those people. Once you're ready to let go, burn that letter.

Day 26: Manage Your Anger

- Exercise. Practice your favorite form of exercise for 15 minutes.
- Practice yoga. You can do some light poses like the mountain pose and Warrior I.
- Practice deep breathing. Breathe deeply for 2 to 3 minutes.
- Take a time-out. Whenever you feel anger building up inside of you, practice mindfulness.

Day 27: Overcome Your Sadness

- Practice transforming your thoughts into positive ones.
- Reach out to loved ones. You may be struggling with feelings of loneliness and an inclination to self-isolate. Make sure to reach out to people who can help you get past this difficult time.
- Care for your inner child. Don't forget to tend to your inner child's needs.

Day 28: Fight the Remorse

- Explore the source of guilt.
- Explain that there's nothing you could've done differently.
- Work on replacing your unhelpful habits with positive ones.

- Consider therapy.

Day 29: Face Your Fears

- Meditate. Meditate for 10 minutes.
- Be an optimist. Expect great things to happen throughout the day.
- Overcome a fear. Take steps toward overcoming a fear.
- Get outside of your comfort zone. Do something you've always wanted to do but couldn't because you doubted your abilities.
- Take chances.

Day 30: Embrace the Healing

Reflect on your inner child's healing journey. How did the past 30 days make you feel? Do you feel like you've changed in any way? Which of the activities mentioned in the challenge are you willing to incorporate into your lifestyle? Which ones are you planning on leaving behind? What steps will you take to maintain your progress?

Conclusion

As you have learned from this book, your inner child represents the culmination of negative emotions hidden in the depths of your soul. By making the child within you happier, you are transforming your soul. Whether this transformation means healing a wounded soul from past trauma, spiritual awakening, or rising to a higher state of spiritual awareness - it's entirely up to you. However, before you start connecting with your inner child, you must understand how it's shaped and how it impacts your life as an adult. You will also have to explore the exact archetype of your inner child - as this can determine your approach to improving your spiritual well-being. Each type has different strengths and weaknesses, so finding out which one lives within you can help you avoid mistakes when trying to form a connection.

Once you know your inner child's archetype, you can move on to learn more about the child's relation to your wounded soul. Understanding your wounded soul is only one of the numerous benefits of discovering your inner child, but it also comes with many challenges. Beyond discovering, exploring your wounded soul also encompasses accepting your inner child with all its positives and negatives. Because while one's inner child has an inherently cheery disposition, traumatic experiences can turn this into a rather somber tone.

Accepting your inner channel means that you've become open to communicating with them and are ready to discover all the ways you can get in touch with your soul. One of the most recommended techniques is meditation. Love-based mindful meditation techniques are particularly known to promote a higher level of spiritual awareness by calming your body and mind and replacing your negative thought processes with loving ones. Journaling is another practice with a positive impact on healing wounded souls. Recording your thoughts and emotions can uncover patterns that indicate a spiritual imbalance.

Of course, there are many other ways to raise your inner child awareness - with many of them pointing towards the best healing paths for your wounded soul. Most of these techniques operate on the same mindfulness principle as meditative exercises do. By simply shifting the attention from your body and mind, they can make you more aware of your soul's needs. That being said, if you're not versed in spirituality, learning most of these techniques will definitely represent some challenges. Fortunately, this book will prepare you for all the possible obstacles you can face during this process by advising you on how to work through them and learn from them when striving for spiritual growth. By overcoming these challenges, you will become much stronger. You will learn how to harvest all the benefits that healing your wounded soul can provide and how to multiply these spiritual gifts.

Last but not least, you will be introduced to the concept of viewing the healing of your inner child as a challenge. Not only is healing the inner child a crucial step towards ensuring spiritual well-being, but by making it into a challenge, you are encouraging yourself to do your best. You can use any of the techniques mentioned in this book or any other mindfulness exercise you can tailor to your needs.

Here's another book by Mari Silva that you might like

Your Free Gift
(only available for a limited time)

Thanks for getting this book! If you want to learn more about various spirituality topics, then join Mari Silva's community and get a free guided meditation MP3 for awakening your third eye. This guided meditation mp3 is designed to open and strengthen ones third eye so you can experience a higher state of consciousness. Simply visit the link below the image to get started.

https://spiritualityspot.com/meditation

References

What is your inner child (and why it's important you get to know them)? (2021, March 26). My Online Therapy. https://myonlinetherapy.com/what-is-your-inner-child-and-why-its-important-you-get-to-know-them/

Davis, S. (n.d.). The wounded inner child. Cptsdfoundation.Org. https://cptsdfoundation.org/2020/07/13/the-wounded-inner-child/

Goldstein, E. (2021, April 6). What is an Inner Child? Integrative Psychotherapy & Trauma Treatment. https://integrativepsych.co/new-blog/what-is-an-inner-child

How to know if you have a wounded inner child (and how to heal). (2021, March 2). The Mighty. https://themighty.com/2021/03/trauma-wounded-inner-child-how-to-know-heal/

Jacobson, S. (2017, March 23). What is the "inner child"? Harley TherapyTM Blog. https://www.harleytherapy.co.uk/counselling/what-is-the-inner-child.htm

Kahn, J. (2019, November 15). Why healing your Inner Child is important. G&STC. https://www.gstherapycenter.com/blog/2019/11/15/why-healing-your-inner-child-is-important

Luna, A. (2019, April 6). 25 signs you have a wounded inner child (and how to heal). LonerWolf. https://lonerwolf.com/feeling-safe-inner-child/

What is inner child work? A guide to healing your inner child. (2020, December 31). Mindbodygreen. https://www.mindbodygreen.com/articles/inner-child-work/

What is your inner child (and why it's important you get to know them). (2021, March 26). My Online Therapy. https://myonlinetherapy.com/what-is-your-inner-child-and-why-its-important-you-get-to-know-them/

The importance of embracing your inner child. (n.d.). Beliefnet.Com. https://www.beliefnet.com/inspiration/articles/the-importance-of-embracing-your-inner-child.aspx

Aquarian. (2019, January 27). Deep dive into the nature child, a primal archetype. Enlighten Up! With The Aquarian. http://www.aquarianonline.com/deep-dive-into-the-nature-child-a-primal-archetype/

Banday, N. (2020, May 4). What is The Child Archetype? - Take a journey into the human psyche. Learn how we operate on a basic level. - Take a journey into the human psyche. Learn how we operate on a basic level. Navigation for Daily Living. https://www.navigationfordailyliving.com/blog/the-child

ChelseaC. (2018, November 9). Find out which of the 6 Child archetypes you fit, and start embracing it. The Odyssey Online. https://www.theodysseyonline.com/whats-my-child-archetype

Couch, S. (2015, August 28). Healing the inner child archetype. Wild Gratitude. https://www.wildgratitude.com/healing-the-inner-child-archetype/

knowyourarchetypes. (2020a, June 23). Child archetype. Know Your Archetypes. https://knowyourarchetypes.com/child-archetype/

knowyourarchetypes. (2020b, August 19). Divine Child Archetype. Know Your Archetypes. https://knowyourarchetypes.com/divine-child-archetype/

knowyourarchetypes. (2020c, August 19). Wounded Child Archetype. Know Your Archetypes. https://knowyourarchetypes.com/wounded-child-archetype/

The child archetype. (2020, February 4). Make A Dent Leadership. https://www.makeadentleadership.com/the-child-archetype/

The "eternal child" function of your personality type - Mystical Analytics. (2021, January 3). Mystical Analytics -. https://mysticalanalytics.com/the-eternal-child-function-of-your-personality-type/

Which Inner Child Archetype are You? (2017, May 23). Jennifer Soldner.

(N.d.). Fcusd.Org. https://www.fcusd.org/cms/lib03/CA01001934/Centricity/Domain/1250/Archetype%20Survey.pdf

Davis, S. (n.d.). Discovering your inner child. Cptsdfoundation.Org. https://cptsdfoundation.org/2020/07/06/discovering-your-inner-child/

Discover your inner child. (2016, October 20). Exploring Your Mind. https://exploringyourmind.com/discover-inner-child/

Giovanis, N. (2021, January 6). Discovering your inner child. A Space Between. https://www.aspacebetween.com.sg/blog/discovering-your-inner-child

Inner child: 6 ways to find yours. (2020, June 26). Healthline. https://www.healthline.com/health/inner-child

Perkal, Z. (2015, April 2). How to find your inner child as an adult. Wanderlust. https://wanderlust.com/journal/find-inner-child/

Roxanne. (2017, April 26). 10 questions to uncover your inner child. TextMyJournal. https://www.textmyjournal.com/10-questions-uncover-inner-child/

Team Zoella. (2022, February 22). How to connect with your inner child to heal, evolve & blossom in adulthood. Zoella. https://zoella.co.uk/2022/02/22/how-to-connect-with-your-inner-child-to-heal-evolve-blossom-in-adulthood/

Neta, N. (2020, October 21). The journey of healing the inner child. Newport Institute. https://www.newportinstitute.com/resources/mental-health/inner-child/

8 tips for healing your inner child. (2021, September 9). Healthline. https://www.healthline.com/health/mental-health/inner-child-healing

Chen, L. (2015, October 19). 7 things your inner child needs to hear you say. Tiny Buddha. https://tinybuddha.com/blog/7-things-your-inner-child-needs-to-hear-you-say/

Coleman, K. (2022, February 23). Why you should embrace your inner child. Her Campus Media. https://www.hercampus.com/school/illinois-state/why-you-should-embrace-your-inner-child/

Embrace Your Inner Child: 5 Ways to embrace your inner child today! (2017, September 8). Girlandtonic.Co.Uk; lauriemcallister. https://girlandtonic.co.uk/embrace-your-inner-child/

Embracing your inner child. (2017, September 14). Nature Explore. https://natureexplore.org/embracing-your-inner-child-2/

Fuller, J. (2018, July 30). Embrace your inner child —. Jane Fuller. https://www.janefuller.co.uk/blog/2018/7/30/embrace-your-inner-child

Meyerowitz, A. (2020, November 20). Why we should embrace our inner child and 5 ways to do it. Red Online. https://www.redonline.co.uk/health-self/self/a34725323/how-to-embrace-inner-child/

www.ingramcontent.com/pod-product-compliance
Lightning Source LLC
Chambersburg PA
CBHW071904090426
42811CB00004B/731
9781638182078